T0146924

NO MORE BEGGARS AND SLAVES

Embracing Our Identity in Christ

ROXANNE MILES

WESTBOW
PRESS®
A DIVISION OF THOMAS NELSON
& ZONDERVAN

WestBow Press books may be ordered through booksellers or by contacting:

WestBow Press
A Division of Thomas Nelson & Zondervan
1663 Liberty Drive
Bloomington, IN 47403
www.westbowpress.com
844-714-3454

Scripture quotations are taken from the Holy Bible, King James Version.

ISBN: 979-8-3850-0739-4 (sc)
ISBN: 979-8-3850-0741-7 (hc)
ISBN: 979-8-3850-0740-0 (e)

Library of Congress Control Number: 2023917497

Print information available on the last page.

WestBow Press rev. date: 09/29/2023

FOREWORD

In her book *No More Beggars and Slaves—Embracing Our Identity in Christ*, Roxanne has captured very well what the title of the book is truly all about. We are living in a time when society battles with the absence of knowing what or where their personal identity comes from, thus destroying so many lives along the way. Even those who are believers in Christ struggle with this concept. Paul's prayer when he spoke to the churches is that "Christ would be formed in you" (Gal. 4:19). When church government functions properly, when pastors take the time to perform their spiritual obligations, and when they learn to delegate authority, true disciples of the Lord will rise up. It is God's will that congregational members who are sitting in the pews grow spiritually. This is the process: moving from a lamb into a sheep; developing from a baby into a mature child of God. In a growth process, believers learn to operate as disciples of the Lord. Roxanne is a prime example of this by the fruit of the gospel she brings forth. It is solid food for all of us believers to grow by. She's exactly what pastors hope to see accomplished in the hearts of those who attend their churches.

Pastor Jann Butler
By His Word Christian Center, Tacoma, WA

INTRODUCTION

It all started over twenty years ago while I was watching *The Lord of the Rings*. Throughout the series, I was drawn to see the strong distinction between royalty and commoners. As the story unfolds, we get an inside view of the members of the Fellowship and the leaders they submitted to or met along the way. Each ruler held much power and responsibility, while most of the people in their kingdoms seemed unaware of or unable to do anything about what was to come. In *The Two Towers*, as the people of Rohan moved into Helm's Deep, God caused me to note how happy the people were to enter the fortress. They saw it as a sanctuary—a place of salvation where they would be protected and safe. Yet as the people entered, they had to find space to sit and lie in the corridors and on the ground—safe but powerless. They remained at the base of the kingdom, while only King Théoden and those of highest rank had access to the upper places, where they could see what was happening and decide the fate of all.

Again, in *The Return of the King*, Gandalf enters the kingdom of Minas Tirith to see the king of Gandor. He rides from the base of the city, up, farther and farther, higher and higher, to where the king resides, passing the commoners along the way. The roads were filled with those who dwelled a long way from the royalty that resided on top.

That was when God impressed upon me why these observations He shared with me mattered. It had little to do with the storyline of *The Lord of the Rings*. The movies only provided a reference to something He wanted me to know—that too many within His kingdom are happy to just be inside the gates of the kingdom. We may all enter the kingdom and acknowledge the King as our own, but what place do we take? We trust the King to rule wisely and fairly and to protect, but do we share in a position of power or influence once we come into the gates?

Beggars and slaves aren't active in creating the outcome of their destiny. They don't move up in rank or sign up for missions that improve their station or the lives of others. They are subject to the will of the king, to the enemy that threatens to attack, to their masters, and to the circumstances they were born into. Their perspective and prospects are limited by their experiences.

It was then God announced to me what His Word makes clear—there are no beggars and slaves in the kingdom of God. No one is meant to lie along the streets waiting to be aided once they enter the pearly gates. There is no one in the kingdom without the ability to speak and act with authority. When God brings us into the kingdom, we come in as sons and daughters and partakers of rights and promises that are reserved for those of royal lineage. As royalty, members of the leading class, we are joint heirs in the work to be done and the victories won.

Since those movies came out (2002–2003), God has given me the opportunity both to be taught and to teach how powerful our perspective is in creating the life we live. He has led me to understand the need to take on and live out the inheritance I have been given. I know I must do more than come into the kingdom and find a quiet and safe place to rest. I must travel up the levels of the kingdom, going deeper in and higher up, to take the position of influence and action He has reserved for His children— confident of whose coat of arms I wear and the kingdom I represent. I hope everyone who reads this book is blessed by the lessons that started that day and continue today. May it allow us all to leave any lingering weak, beggarly, and binding thoughts behind so we can confidently sit in the seat reserved for us in the kingdom of God!

DEDICATION

To Pastor, Lady G, the Legacy Ladies, Brother Wayne, and Sister Toni.
Thank you for pushing me, leading me,
encouraging me, and journeying with me.
Without you, this book would not have been possible.

CHAPTER 1

WHO I THINK I AM

We spend much of our lives discovering who we are—what we like, what we can do, and how others see us. From early on, our identity gets crafted by what we are told about ourselves and what we tell ourselves about our abilities and character. Our ongoing internal dialogue results in deep-rooted views of self. Scholars have long held a nature-versus-nurture debate on whether our pedigree or life experiences most influence our personality and behaviors. We could all likely look back to see how both family and what we have been through have contributed to our view of the world. Yet when we became Christians, our identity, the fact of being who or what a person or thing is, was changed. Regeneration (a change in our spirit) led to an awakening of a new reality in our design, a new identity, and a marvelous opportunity to embrace the way our Father God sees us and made us to be. He saw us when we were "yet in our mother's womb" and proclaimed us fearfully and wonderfully made (Ps. 139:13–14) from the beginning of our existence, yet, somehow, we struggle with seeing ourselves with His eyes. We tend to continue relating to life through our natural eyes which are trained on what we have always seen, focused on our past and failures, instead of putting on lenses that reveal and embrace our new spiritual identity in Christ.

While we know that our identity changed somehow when we received salvation through grace, we don't always realize how it changed. Scripture holds the answer, but truth must be sought out and revealed to us by the Spirit. If we don't seek a new view, our vision of self remains limited and shaded, pulling the color and clarity out of whom God created us to be.

Scripture opens the door to the revelation of how our identity changes through the gift of salvation:

> Galatians 4:9: But now, after that ye have known God, or rather are known of God, how turn ye again to the weak and beggarly elements, whereunto ye desire again to be in bondage?

Note this scripture starts with "After that ye have known God, or rather are known of God." We often pass over the simpler words in scripture, like "to know"; however, to know God is a deep experience. When we become alive in Christ, we get to know God in more personal, meaningful ways than when He was simply an idea to us. And as we get to know God, we learn more about who we are in relationship to Him. Our concept of self is often based on roles—mother, sister, friend, husband, child—and we enter into a new relationship and role with God upon salvation. Living with God as Father and in fellowship with the Son and Spirit creates new dynamics in our lives. Salvation creates such a powerful, major change in us; we must recognize that our knowledge and identity in Him will change drastically as well as we get to know Him more and know more of who He is in and for us. The word known (GK: *ginosko*) has many dimensions. It means *to know in all contexts and applications*. In Christ, there isn't a time, place, or circumstance when we shouldn't consider ourselves to know God or be known by Him. To know is to be fully aware of, to feel, to have knowledge of, and to understand with such intimacy that we can perceive even more than is physically before us. We know it fully in our minds, in our hearts, and in our spirit. When we know God, we come to know Him even more deeply through the following ways:

- From past experiences. We have a history that helps us understand His will and purpose for us *personally.*
- From discernment. We are able to come to examine His nature by reason, study, and meditation based on information that is found in scripture.
- From hearing from others. We can learn from another's disclosure of what He has done in their lives. He is not a respecter of persons (Acts 10:34).

- From observations leading to perception. We come to know what to expect from Him and perceive what He is doing, even in new situations and circumstances, because the Holy Spirit in us shares an unction of what God is trying to reveal or accomplish in our lives through the situation.

When we first become aware of God as young believers, our "knowing" is made up of a stream of new information or revelation that helps bring an understanding of spiritual things into our lives. Over time, our goal is to know God in a more complete sense—in all contexts and applications, from all sides, and without questions or gaps in knowledge. We want to know what He is thinking and feeling and what His desires for us are personally. That is the journey this book focuses on. By knowing God and our identity in Him even more, we can:

- Have an immediate recognition of God's will and plan in our lives through a strong familiarity with Him.
- Confess that God is exactly who and what He professes to be in scripture, and what that means for each of us, through the new identity He provides us.
- Acknowledge and confirm the truth of who He is by being who and what He has enabled us to be.

Galatians 4 asks us a very direct question: *How can we know God and turn back again to the weak and beggarly elements and again desire to be in bondage?*

Scripture is good at recognizing the limitations of our natural identity, which ruled our self-image and human condition before salvation. Our natural elements included weakness, being beggarly, and living in bondage. Our human nature and self-image continue to hold these elements in position as our routine way of thinking if they are not challenged and replaced by new thoughts (Isa. 55:8–9). His thoughts are different from our thoughts but they are not beyond our realm of understanding, if we choose to pursue them.

Ephesians 2:2–3 says that prior to Christ's redemption, we walked according to the world and according to the flesh; we were children of wrath. That was *before* being born again (John 3), *before* becoming a new creature (2 Cor. 5:17), *before* being saved by grace (Eph. 2:8). That was our previous condition, our old way of thinking, believing, and acting. Yet while our spiritual condition has been changed by regeneration (an entire change in the inner being of a person that God produces in us), we often still look at the world from the old identity that is anchored in the flesh—what we see, touch, smell, hear, and taste. If we don't challenge our thoughts, we remain anchored in what we know to be true based on old desires, needs, and experiences, which are limited by our human capacities. When this occurs:

- We will continue to see ourselves as beggars who are trying to receive something more—even though God has already given us everything we need.
- We will continue to see ourselves as slaves, bound by sin and subject to bondage.
- We will continue to see ourselves as weak against temptation and the challenges of this world.

If we continue to relate to life out of our old identity, we won't experience everything God has established for us to receive as part of our new one. The old is meant to pass away continually, a process we either help or hinder through our mindset. Transformation in thinking will move slowly or quickly based on how well we know God and pursue spiritual truth. We are charged with renewing our minds to the spiritual reality of who we are in Christ. When we do so, we are able to prove (live out for all to see) the good, acceptable, and perfect will God has for our lives.

> Romans 12:1–2: I beseech you therefore, brethren, by the mercies of God, that ye present your bodies a living sacrifice, holy, acceptable unto God, which is your reasonable service. And be not conformed to this world: but be ye transformed by the renewing of your mind, that ye may prove what is that good, and acceptable, and perfect, will of God.

To be weak (GK: *asthenes*) is to be without strength, to be feeble and impotent. Do we sometimes still feel that way?

To be beggarly (GK: *prosaiteo*) is to solicit repeatedly and excessively to attempt to gain. It implies approaching another with an expectation that help can be found while understanding that we have no right or guarantee to receive it. Might we be asking God repeatedly for things that He has already given us the right to access on our own?

To be in bondage (GK: *douleuo*) is to be enslaved, held to involuntary service, and made subject to a law or master. Are there influences that hold us captive and keep us from experiencing the liberty of God's love, peace, and joy?

> Galatians 4:9: But now, after that ye have known God, or rather are known of God, how turn ye again to the weak and beggarly elements, whereunto ye desire again to be in bondage?

Elements (GK: *stoicheion*) are fundamental principles or rudimentary beliefs. They are the most basic concepts that make up our thinking. If thoughts of weakness, unmet needs, and overwhelming temptations are persistently part of how we think of ourselves, we have not yet embraced a new identity in Christ. When we look in the mirror, what do we say to ourselves? What do we base this opinion on? If they are negative thoughts of weakness, how are those thoughts undermining all we say and do each day?

With our new identity, we are given the opportunity and responsibility to think differently. Once we embrace who we are in Christ, we can then think the way scripture charges us to think. We can begin to receive, believe, and act on the thoughts God has about and for us. When this occurs:

- We will have a sound mind, which recognizes love and power but not fear (2 Tim. 1:7).
- We will think on things that are true, honest, just, pure, and lovely; are of good report; are of virtue; and lead to praise (Phil. 4:8).
- We will be strong and courageous no matter the situation or circumstance (Josh. 1:9).

Our identity in Christ makes us rich in many new and tangible ways, not beggars.

Our identity in Christ makes us masters of our destiny, not slaves.

Our identity in Christ makes us strong and courageous rulers and ambassadors who carry the authority of the King.

Seeking knowledge about and fully embracing our spiritual identity is the key to living the life of abundance that God has established for us to live. If we fail to do so, we risk "turning back again" to live a life grounded only in our natural limitations, in lack and in weakness . We will live each day according to who we used to be, instead of approaching each day as God created, called, and empowered us to be.

> Galatians 4:1-9: Now I say, that the heir, as long as he is a child, differs nothing from a servant, though he be lord of all; but is under tutors and governors until the time appointed of the father. Even so we, when we were children, were in bondage under the elements of the world: But when the fulness of the time was come, God sent forth his Son, made of a woman, made under the law, to redeem them that were under the law, that we might receive the adoption of sons. And because ye are sons, God hath sent forth the Spirit of his Son into your hearts, crying, Abba, Father. Wherefore thou art no more a servant, but a son; and if a son, then an heir of God through Christ. Howbeit then, when ye knew not God, ye did service unto them which by nature are no gods. But now, after that ye have known God, or rather are known of God, how turn ye again to the weak and beggarly elements, whereunto ye desire again to be in bondage?

Reflection Questions

Where has your concept of self-come from?

How much have you invested in developing your knowledge of your spiritual identity in Christ?

How is your spiritual identity reflected

- in your life every day?
- in times of trouble?
- in your use of time?
- in your self-talk?
- in your interactions with others?

CHAPTER 2

I Am Royalty

When we were born into our natural family, we entered this world subject to the genes (DNA) of our biological parents, and then our values and thoughts were shaped by those who raised us. As we noted in the last chapter, these things, as well as life experiences and our view of self that developed out of those experiences, have a powerful influence on how we see ourselves and live our lives.

When we are born again, born a second time of the Spirit through Christ, we are birthed into a new family—a family with a Father and with its own values and ways of influencing our thoughts and decisions. Similarly, our spiritual identity arises and becomes known to us in much the same manner our natural identity formed—over time, by influence and through experience.

> John 3:1–9: There was a man of the Pharisees, named Nicodemus, a ruler of the Jews: The same came to Jesus by night, and said unto him, Rabbi, we know that thou art a teacher come from God: for no man can do these miracles that thou does, except God be with him. Jesus answered and said unto him, Verily, verily, I say unto thee, *except a man be born again, he cannot see the kingdom of God.* Nicodemus saith unto him, how can a man be born when he is old? Can he enter the second time into his mother's womb, and be born? Jesus answered, Verily, verily, I say unto thee, except a man be born of water and

of the Spirit, he cannot enter into the kingdom of God. That which is born of the flesh is flesh; and *that which is born of the Spirit is spirit*. Marvel not that I said unto thee, Ye must be born again.

Once birthed into the kingdom of God, our spiritual possibilities and identity change because we can see things that we never saw before. We are now being taught things we previously could never comprehend. While the natural identity may remain the same, we inherited the capacity to become new (2 Cor. 5:17). We were placed in a new family with new brothers and sisters whom we now grow up together with. With this introduction into the family of God, we also inherit shared resources and responsibilities that go along with being part of a family—chores are assigned, we learn from those older than us, we care for those younger than us, and we also learn to respect the knowledge and discipline offered by the Father. We are charged to grow up in this family, like we did our natural family, and to reflect certain values and pass down family traditions and wisdom. We have reason to celebrate this spiritual family even more when we consider that it is rich, powerful, loving, influential, and destined for greatness—well beyond the limitations of our physical family. This family has everything we need, and our experience within it is centered on how well we understand, accept, and embrace our place within it.

Galatians 4:1–9: Now I say that the heir, as long as he is a child, differs nothing from a servant, though he be lord of all; but is under tutors and governors until the time appointed of the father. Even so we, when we were children, were in bondage under the elements of the world: But when the fulness of the time was come, God sent forth his Son, made of a woman, made under the law, To redeem them that were under the law, that *we might receive the adoption of sons*. And because ye are sons, God hath *sent forth the Spirit of his Son into your hearts*, crying, Abba, Father. Wherefore *thou art no more a servant, but a son; and if a son, then an heir of God through Christ*. Howbeit then, when ye knew not God, ye did service unto them which by nature are no gods. But now, after that ye have known God, or rather are known of God, how turn ye again to the weak and beggarly elements, whereunto ye desire again to be in bondage?

In Galatians 4:1, we learned that we are potential heirs as soon as we join the family of God. An heir (GK: *kleronomos*) is one who gets privileges, rights, resources, and power by apportionment from the current legal holder of those things. We become a sharer of all that the kingdom holds when we are adopted (placed) into this new familial position because of the new birth. Our new position is sonship. This is a gender-neutral term that positions one under the care and authority of the Father through our placement into the household of the kingdom of God.

While we come into the kingdom as sons and daughters, we must look deeper to fully understand how we come to hold the portion of inheritance God has promised us. "Now I say, that the heir, as long as he is a child, differs nothing from a servant, though he be lord of all, but is under tutors and governors until the time appointed of the father." In this case, the term *child* refers to an infant—one who is simple-minded, immature, and not of age. While the child has a position in the family, the child is subject to nannies, tutors, and those who do not belong to the family but who serve it until the child gets old enough to understand what it means to be an heir and to act accordingly. While there may be many children born into a royal family, normally only one is identified as heir to the throne. To our benefit, God *invites and positions us all as heirs through Christ*, but we must *grow* into maturity so we can fully access and live out our inheritance. God, the Father, is the decider on when and how to pass the benefits of the inheritance on—and He is looking for those ready to use what He provides well. We see some of this reflected in the parable of the Prodigal Son (Luke 15:11–32). The father allowed a son to go off and waste his inheritance, while the other son stayed close and served the family interests, knowing that he had immediate access to all the family had and would receive even more as family knowledge, reputation, and assets passed to him over the years. While the Prodigal Son was welcomed home, he missed out on a long period of relationship with the father; he missed out on the daily ability to grow and benefit from being at home with the father. He wasted away the inheritance instead of storing it or using it for the life of abundance the father desired him to have.

Galatians 4 teaches us that our hearts, now filled with the Spirit, cry out, "Abba, Father," pulling us into the relationship of sonship. God is many things—Creator and Sustainer—but He called us to have this father-son relationship with Him as well The Spirit pulls us toward our spiritual position and identity in Christ—as we are now dear to, developed by, subject to, and responsible to a Father who loves us and knows how to best care for us. As we journey to know God in all of His many aspects of Fatherhood, we can see our position in sonship more clearly as a child of the Most High, as a son or daughter in the house of the Father. The position and relationship of sonship is necessary for understanding and accessing the inheritance He alone can provide. From Galatians and the Prodigal Son, we learn that the father alone determines the time and means of apportionment. He releases more of the inheritance when the child is ready to receive it and use it well for the benefit of the family.

Are we ready to move from being children to heirs who understand the rights, responsibilities, and benefits of the position given to us upon coming into the family of God?

As we do, we will become more and more aware of the power of who we are and who we were designed to be as His children. We will also realize that with "much power comes much responsibility." We can see this in the physical world from watching people who hold titles of royalty. Their identity is not only for themselves; they also represent a king/queen and a kingdom. They both protect and advance the throne of the ruler. They protect the boundaries of the kingdom from the enemy and find ways to use their wealth and power for the benefit of all those they are responsible for. In short, the inheritance God puts in our hands is not just for us; it is to be used wisely to have a good effect on His kingdom. He gives to all His children, desiring we demonstrate joy and maturity in the receiving by honoring our place in the kingdom in which we belong and charging us to protect and serve family, and kingdom, interests.

As we grow as spiritual children, we are to reflect the image of our Father God (show *His* DNA) more; we are to mature in thinking, speaking, and acting out the family values we read in the Word. His influence causes us to transform by renewing our minds, disciplining our will, and redirecting our emotions. As we mature, we are better able to identify which elements within us (the weak and beggarly) need to be challenged and removed from our thoughts so we can walk as heirs who represent the kingdom of God in every situation. We come to understand that we represent the Father and His kingdom through the way we carry ourselves each day and especially when confronted by His enemy, who is able to make this world difficult for all who dwell in it. This persona of strength is part of the spiritual identity that comes out of a close relationship with the King of kings and Lord of lords. It is a title that we should "affirm constantly" by how we view, speak, and act as representatives of our Father—and this especially applies in how we see and treat ourselves.

> Titus 3:6–8: Which he shed on us abundantly through Jesus Christ our Savior; that being justified by his grace, *we should be made heirs* according to the hope of eternal life. This is a faithful saying, and these things *I will that thou affirm constantly*, that they which have believed in God might be careful to maintain good works. These things are good and profitable unto men.

> Hebrews 1:1–3: God, who at sundry times and in divers manners spoke in time past unto the fathers by the prophets, hath in these last days spoken unto us by his Son, *whom he hath appointed heir of all things*, by whom also he made the worlds; Who being the brightness of his glory, and the express image of his person, and upholding all things by the word of his power, when he had by himself purged our sins, sat down on the right hand of the Majesty on high.

> Romans 8:16–18: The *Spirit itself bears witness with our spirit*, that we are the children of God: And *if children, then heirs; heirs of God, and joint-heirs with Christ*; if so be that we suffer with him, that we may be also glorified together. For I reckon that the sufferings of this present

time are not worthy to be compared with the glory which
shall be revealed in us.

We know that *Christ is the reason for our access to any inheritance.*
He is the Son that the Father has given all things to, but our Father has
chosen to make us joint heirs with the Son. Joint heirs participate in
common; Christ shares his lot with us, and we only receive through and
with him. What he has rights to, we have rights to. What he has been
given, we can share in. What he commands, we can command through
our relationship and position in him. Of course, we also share the same
purpose and representation of the kingdom Christ did, now as children
and ambassadors (2 Cor. 5:2), who speak of the matters of the family with
authority, inviting others to know, understand, and see the kingdom of
God and what it stands for as well. This position is permanent, complete,
and comes with all the benefits and responsibilities Christ demonstrated
to us while he walked among us in human form (Phil. 2:1–8).

When we were appointed (GK: *tithemi*) into sonship, we were given
a place and position in God's kingdom that *only* goes to His sons and
daughters. Think of it as a legal action which has resulted in us being
officially added as a beneficiary in the "will" of the Father. All the shared
inheritance He has set aside for apportionment to those who believe is
called out in the New Testament; it is an inheritance only made accessible
to His children. It is by reviewing the Word of God that we find the *will*
of God and learn who we are and what conditions He has included for us
to receive our apportionment of the inheritance.

Have you heard that we, as heirs, have been raised up to *sit together
with Christ in heavenly places* (Eph. 2:6)? Think of that position. Can you
see yourself humbly seated with Christ, where the earth is His footstool,
with angels ready to respond at any moment to the Lord's command,
and with the full storehouse of God in the background? While we know
that Christ belongs there because of His nature and sacrifice, we have the
privilege of knowing that we were raised to that place as well because we
are joint heirs in Him—while Christ was the first, we are added sons and
daughters. *He sacrificed to give us that view, so let's pause to take it in!* The
more we can see the world (his footstool) and ourselves (joint heirs) from
that position, the more we are able to understand our spiritual authority

and identity in Christ. We say "in Christ" a lot; the phrase is abundant in the New Testament, yet we don't always hold the mindset of being "in Christ" in our daily lives. I challenge you to think of "in Christ" as being "with Christ." As a joint heir, see yourself seated, standing and walking out each day with the one who never fears, never doubts, and knows all things will work for our good in God's appointed time. You are always with Him as a permanent member of the family; you have a position of honor that doesn't change and gives you access to so many things—now you just need to grow into knowing what to do with the power, authority, wealth, and responsibilities of the kingdom you have been adopted and placed into "in and with" Christ!

We know the Lord is the possessor, owner, master of all property and people (Rom. 11:36). He is the head of the church. He has complete authority over all things. Stop and ponder again what we *absolutely know* about God and Jesus, the Christ. Take time to let awe and wonder form in our hearts over their majesty, dominion, and power. And then let our hearts and minds absorb that, somehow, through God's amazing grace, we are joint heirs to His kingdom and this authority. Where Christ goes, we will go. What He has, we have access to. Consider that we, as heirs, even as children, can overcome great things in this world because of the greatness we have by being born into the family of God with access to all the provision and strength of God's house (1 John 4:4).

> 2 Corinthians 10:7–8: Do ye look on things after the outward appearance? If any man trust to himself that *he is Christ's*, let him of himself think this again, that, as he is Christ's, even so are we Christ's. For though I should boast somewhat more of *our authority, which the Lord hath given us for edification*, and not for your destruction, I should not be ashamed.

God's last will and testament, His Word, defines the powerful, distinct, and unique spiritual position we have been given that comes with our spiritual identity as an heir. While God does not give us His throne, nor Christ's seat directly (Lucifer's vanity made him want to take it), *we are joint heirs who have access to all He has, right now, here on earth and not just in eternity*. Will we want to run off, like the Prodigal Son, and use it for our own gain, or do we have the mind of an heir, the mind of Christ, where we feel the weight of the responsibility to use all that is available to us for the good of the kingdom? Are we prepared to share not only in the glory, wealth, and peace but also, on occasion, in the suffering, experiencing pain jointly, or the same type of pain as Christ had to, to bring His kingdom to a fallen world? Being an heir has wonderful benefits, but it also requires accountability for the power given. We must not misuse or bury it. We only need to look at the parable of the talents (Matt. 25) to know the weight of the responsibility of how we must thoughtfully use the spiritual gifts and abilities we were given to explore and reveal our spiritual identity. We need to listen, learn, and mature in things of the kingdom, so the Father can grant fuller apportionment of the inheritance to us now, in the future, and into eternity. After all, *our understanding and management of our inheritance on earth will have an impact on what is entrusted to us when we are absent from this body and present with the Lord.*

> Luke 12:48: From everyone who has been given much, much will be demanded; and from the one who has been entrusted with much, much more will be asked.

While the charge of sonship may feel daunting and overwhelming at times, we have to remember that we are joint heirs. It means what we do and what we have, we do *together with Christ*. He is with us to share life's sufferings, those that happen within this fallen world, as well as give us access to a greater array of solutions and privileges that can change circumstances (before) and outcomes (after) every situation. The rise and fall of life's events don't change our spiritual identity—we must take our position, shift our perspective to take in the view from Christ's vantage point, and strategize how we will conquer in partnership with our Lord and King when confronted by the enemy. We are not weak, beggarly, or enslaved to fear or any other master—no heir of the One True Living God ever is.

So, now that we know (a task that requires study, meditation, and acceptance) the power of our rebirth into the family of God, we must spend time each day exploring what it means to be an heir of God and

15

learning what He has set aside as our inheritance, as it is the foundation of our spiritual identity in Christ. It's time for us to step into our sonship and learn how to read "the will and testament" of God and position ourselves for apportionment of our inheritance. Here's a great place to start:

> Galatians 3:28–29: There is neither Jew nor Greek, there is neither bond nor free, there is neither male nor female: for ye are all one in Christ Jesus. And if ye be Christ's, then are ye *Abraham's seed, and heirs according to the promise.*

> James 2:4–5: Are ye not then partial in yourselves, and are become judges of evil thoughts? Hearken, my beloved brethren, hath not God chosen the poor of this world *rich in faith*, and *heirs of the kingdom* which he hath promised to them that love him?

Our inheritance is granted through and by faith. We become an offspring of Abraham once *the seed of faith has been sown into us to believe in Christ* as our Lord (Rom. 10:9–10). God promised Abraham that there would be a multitude that would follow him, finding access to spiritual privilege and blessings (a huge inheritance) through faith.

> Hebrews 11:8–12: By faith Abraham, *when called to go to a place he would later receive as his inheritance, obeyed and went,* even though he did not know where he was going. By faith he made his home in the promised land like a stranger in a foreign country; he lived in tents, as did Isaac and Jacob, who were heirs with him of the same promise. For he was looking forward to the city with foundations, whose architect and builder is God. And by faith even Sarah, who was past childbearing age, was enabled to bear children because she considered him faithful who had made the promise. And so from this one man, and he as good as dead, came descendants as numerous as the stars in the sky and as countless as the sand on the seashore.

Abraham showed us what it means to be *heirs according to a promise.*

He taught us that we must take action to possess the promise that was given. The action we take is the sign that we have faith—confidence and assurance—that something unseen to us now will eventually be seen in this world. Like Abraham, we are often directed to go into foreign or unknown lands and situations, to take a bold step without all the information we need to feel confident—which is exactly why faith must provide the assurance one needs to believe and act. When physical circumstances do not produce confidence, we must turn to our understanding and faith in spiritual promises to find it.

Throughout God's Word, there are many promises given to His heirs, who understand that they must possess their inheritance through faith. A promise (GK: *epaggelia*) is an announcement or pledge with divine assurances. It is a statement of the *benefits available* through sonship, yet it is important to know that *promises must be collected upon* to be received. He has made the pledge—a verbal commitment—which someone needs to take action to claim as belonging to them. Think of the blessings sitting in a savings deposit box. We have been given the key, but we must go to the box and open it through an act of faith, knowing God has placed what is promised inside. Faith creates a confident assurance that what we find will bring something spiritual, new, powerful, and effective to the situation. And we build this confidence on one important fact—it is impossible for God, our Father, to lie to His children about what He has declared our inheritance to be.

> Hebrews 6:16–18: For men verily swear by the greater: and an oath for confirmation is to them an end of all strife. Wherein God, willing more abundantly *to shew unto the heirs of promise the immutability (unchanging nature) of his counsel*, confirmed it by an oath: That by two immutable things, in which it was *impossible for God to lie*, we might have a strong consolation, who have fled for refuge to lay hold upon the hope set before us.

Are you ready to take steps to embrace your place in the royal family today—to live as a joint heir with Christ, ready to learn more about the inheritance that is promised and ready to receive it by faith? If so, then read on—chapter 3 awaits!

Reflection Questions

Did you learn anything new about being a child of God from this chapter? How can you deepen the parent-child relationship with Him?

What aspects of your spiritual inheritance did you already know about?

What parts of your inheritance do you want to learn more about?

What can you do with this information to build a stronger spiritual identity as one who does everything "with" and "in" Christ who is sharing His position with you as joint heir?

CHAPTER 3

NO BEGGIN', JUST BELIEVIN'

As heirs of the King, we have so much available to us, yet beggarly thoughts can still linger and influence our lifestyle. In simple terms, being beggarly is to have to ask for something we need from others who have no obligation to give, even if they have it. A beggar has no resources of their own, so they rely on soliciting from others until the request(s) has resulted in some form of gain or the beggar tires of asking. Everything the beggar needs is held by others, and they have no rights to receive it. This generates an attitude of lack—which is not the mindset of abundance and gratitude that is part of our Christian inheritance.

Being beggarly is more than just having to make the request or ask. It starts with a stream of thought on the lack in one's life and limited means to resolve it. Regularly thinking on unmet needs forms a situation where we can become very focused on what we don't have. These thoughts fixate on our personal limitations and create uncertainty in our lives. Even if we have resources for some or even most things in our lives, we can still have a beggarly mindset regarding the things that feel out of reach or that we have no choice but to rely on others for. We can put control of getting our needs met into someone else's hands—and let fear, bitterness, or anger grow if they don't provide. This can also lead to hoarding or being miserly with what we do have, being unable to share or give with any form of generosity because we don't know if and when we ourselves will next receive.

A beggarly mindset has three conditions:

1. Lack of one's own personal possessions or ability to meet one's own needs.
2. The need to ask others, often unknown to us, for what is needed without confidence of receiving.
3. A life focused on the needs of self, without the capacity to care for or share generously with others.

When we take a look at these elements and how they relate to our spiritual identity, we should quickly realize that beggarly thoughts do not belong to an heir of the King of kings and Lord of lords. We have vastly more abilities through Christ, we know the greatest giver of all time, and God calls us to faith, which inherently includes confidence and assurance in receiving what we currently do not have but hope for (Heb. 11:1–3). Let's look at the first of the three parts of the beggarly mindset we want to overcome:

Eliminating misconceptions of our lack of possessions
and inability to meet our needs.

The mind is a powerful tool. An overemphasis on what we don't have or can't do can overshadow what we do have and what is possible in our lives. God knew that the limitations of our physical identity and natural circumstances could be blinding to us (2 Pet. 1:8–10), which is why scripture is full of descriptions of what we *do* have and what *is* possible with Christ. If we ever doubt it, we must return to our heavenly place seated with Christ and take a good look around! The sky is no longer the limit.

The list of our possessions is long—love (Rom. 5:5), forgiveness and redemption (Eph. 1:7), peace (John 14:27), strength (Phil. 4:13), to name just a few. Yet, even though heirs have an abundance of inherited possessions, abilities, and rights written in the will, we miss out on them if the will has never been opened, studied, revealed to us, nor the riches contained within it accepted. While a child of God, we may still need to "come of age" to fully embrace and receive the apportionment our Father has set aside for us. Too often, we remain a babe in the family of God—one who hasn't grown up or taken the steps to be eligible to receive and manage what they have been given.

Learning and embracing knowledge of what we have waiting for us and knowledge of how to possess it can quickly change our mindset from lack toward one of wanting to understand how to access new means of abundance through heirship. Even if something is not "in hand" at the moment, having knowledge that it exists and that it is a possession set apart for the children of God brings a revelation of what we have current or future access to.

The will and testament of Jesus Christ outlines the heart of God and His design to make us part of His kingdom. When we step into that realization, our minds can shift toward a knowledge of provision and abundance compared to lack because our position gives us access to more than we can physically see or currently hold. There is more abundance for us in this life, through Jesus making us joint heirs to the promises and provision of God, the Father, than what is in our bank accounts or emotional storehouse. Abundance given by God is not just limited to the "afterlife" with Christ in eternity. His goodness is for us today, here in the "land of the living."

> John 10:10: The thief does not come except to steal, and to kill, and to destroy. I have come that they may have life, and that they *may have it more abundantly.*

So, if our inheritance in Christ includes abundance, where does it come from? How do we experience it in our lives today?

We have been given talents, gifts, and abilities to gain what we need for our "daily bread." There is a pathway that our Father has established for each of us to pursue for our needs to be met through actions taken on our own behalf. Our human nature is anchored by a fearful and wonderful design (Ps. 139:14) and God-given talents (Matt. 25:14–28) distributed as God wills. In the parable of the talents, God gave to each according to their ability, with an expectation that each does something for him/herself and the kingdom with what they had been given. Jeremiah 29:11 also assures us that God put thoughtful consideration not only into our design but also into a plan for each of His children's futures, which gives us a hope—something to look forward to with great anticipation. This is why John was able to write to the brethren with a very strong sentiment, charging us to invest in our soul—our thinking, our choices, how we feel about ourselves and God—as a means of accessing greater prosperity and abundance in life.

> 3 John 1:2–3: Beloved, I pray that you may prosper in all things and be in health, just as your soul prospers. For I rejoiced greatly when brethren came and testified of the truth that is in you, just as you walk in the truth.

Seeking the truth of who we are in Christ is a worthy journey of exploration. The more we embrace the unique design that is who we are and put those elements to good use in the world and for God's kingdom, the quicker we can release the flow of abundance in our lives. By using what we have been given to make an impact on this world, we will both receive the benefits of the work of our hands (an income or provision) and be able to bring forth glory for God's kingdom, showing we are ready to be heirs and not just children that others take care of both within and outside the kingdom.

Are you holding back on realizing how talented, capable, strong, influential, and effective you are designed and empowered to be? Are you putting yourself in situations where your wonderful design can be revealed to generate provision in your life *and* bring God glory?

By taking the talents given by God and putting them to work, we show God that we have embraced *the gift of being us*. We are here because the world needs to receive what we have to give, the way only we can give it. This shouldn't be intimidating because we aren't in bondage to our personal weakness and limitations. We have access to the riches in glory and grace, and to all the strength, power, and influence set aside for His heirs. We have strength beyond our own inside us and flowing from above. Throughout scripture, the inspired writers of God continuously prayed that each believer would be filled with wisdom and revelation to know and understand the hope, riches, and greatness we have in Christ. Why does this concept continue to come forth, time and again, to offer us assurances? Because we all need extra support to combat fear. We need this charge to learn and live out our spiritual identity through an intentional decision not to let our physical identity and insecurities get in the way of us being who we were meant to be or to keep us from doing the things we were called to do. Too often, we focus on what we cannot do, the risks of doing it, or what we lack in ability, strength, and knowledge. We compare ourselves to others and take a step back, instead of forward. Our self-concept and self-confidence are limited; they keep us from being bold, which is exactly what fulfilling our spiritual identity requires. Pray today, and every day, that our knowledge of our spiritual identity built on our position and possessions as heirs of God would continue to grow into a strength and boldness that is beyond what we have ever considered for ourselves. This will empower us to change our thoughts from lack to life—and life more abundant!

> Ephesians 1:17–19: That the God of our Lord Jesus Christ, the Father of glory, may give to you the spirit of wisdom and revelation in the knowledge of Him, the eyes of your understanding being enlightened; *that you may know what is the hope of His calling, what are the riches of the glory of His inheritance in the saints, and what is the exceeding greatness of His power toward us who believe,* according to the working of His mighty power.

> Colossians 1:9–12: For this reason we also, since the day we heard it, do not cease to pray for you, and to ask that *you may be filled with the knowledge of His will in all wisdom and spiritual understanding; that you may walk worthy of the Lord, fully pleasing Him, being fruitful in every good work and increasing in the knowledge of God; strengthened with all might, according to His glorious power,* for all patience and longsuffering with joy; giving thanks to the Father *who has qualified us to be partakers of the inheritance of the saints* in the light.

His grace conveys salvation. It makes us whole and complete in everything that we need to do "exceedingly abundantly above" what we can imagine when we rely on our own strength. Salvation (GK: *sozo*) is to save, deliver, protect, heal, preserve, enable to do well, and make whole. If there is any part of us that isn't complete, if there are elements of our lives that feel as though they have lack or that we aren't doing well in, those are the areas that we turn into partnership and joint heirship with Christ "to make whole." That is where we must look to find what God has made available to us, for us to fill every gap and close every wound. His grace (GK: *charis*) is the divine act of giving us unmerited or undeserved things that we cannot provide for ourselves. He puts this divine influence on our hearts to turn toward Him and receive the things that are missing in our lives, to bring forward the completeness and abundance that is promised to those who have accepted the gift of living in fellowship with Him. Never hesitate to turn to Him when a lack or a gap appears, to invite the power of Christ and the authority and provision of the kingdom He shares with us to come into our lives.

> 2 Corinthians 12:9: And he said unto me, My grace is sufficient for thee: for *my strength is made perfect in weakness*. Most gladly therefore will I rather glory in my infirmities, that the power of Christ may rest upon me.

> Ephesians 3:20–21: Now to Him who is *able to do exceedingly abundantly above all that we ask or think, according to the power that works in us*, to Him be glory in the church by Christ Jesus to all generations, forever and ever. Amen.

While we each have a robust array of our own God-given abilities and heaven's storehouse at our disposal, having access to God's wealth and inheritance doesn't always mean that we will have everything we want at every moment, but it does ensure that access to the family's wealth exists for the things the Father has established as His will to provide us. The riches He opens to us are a means to an end and not the goal itself. The goal is not to acquire wealth or to focus one's life on the pursuit of achieving more of it, as one cannot serve two masters (Matt. 6:24). We know that God will always provide what is necessary to meet the needs of His child, especially when the will of the child is to serve the kingdom of God with it.

1 Timothy 6:17–19: Charge them that are rich in this world, that they be not high-minded, nor trust in uncertain riches, but in the living God, who giveth us richly all things to enjoy; *that they do good, that they be rich in good works, ready to distribute, willing to communicate*; laying up in store for themselves a good foundation against the time to come, that they may lay hold on eternal life.

Philippians 4:19: But my God shall *supply all your need according to his riches in glory* by Christ Jesus.

Luke 16:10–12: He who is faithful in what is least is faithful also in much; and he who is unjust in what is least is unjust also in much. Therefore, if you have not been faithful in the unrighteous mammon, who will commit to your trust the true riches? And if you have not been faithful in what is another man's, who will give you what is your own?

Accessing the kingdom's riches starts with us establishing our intent and commitment to the kingdom of God. Seek first the kingdom of God and be confident that *all other things that we need* to fulfill that intent can and will be added unto us (Matt. 6:33).

While God has shown through scripture that He has no desire for us to be in a beggarly condition, we see that several people *begged of Christ* to receive healing. These examples reveal to us that while the people making the request had no way to fulfill their needs, they made a *personal, selective, and expectant request* of Jesus, knowing that He was key to accessing more resources than they possessed. They had a recognition that He alone could and would meet their needs and then put their confidence into action—demonstrating recognition that His abundance and strength were available to them. They didn't wait on a corner for a passerby, they didn't simply hope an answer would come to them one day; they sought Him out. They said and did bold things borne of an expectation that He was the source of a spiritual solution available to them because of their choice to know Him.

Mark 5:22–29: And behold, one of the rulers of the synagogue came, Jairus by name. And when he saw Him, he fell at His feet and begged Him earnestly, saying, "My little daughter lies at the point of death. *Come and lay Your hands on her, that she may be healed,* and she will live." So Jesus went with him, and a great multitude followed Him and thronged Him. Now a certain woman had a flow of blood for twelve years and had suffered many things from many physicians. She had spent all that she had and was no better, but rather grew worse. When she heard about Jesus, she came behind Him in the crowd and touched His garment. *For she said, "If only I may touch His clothes, I shall be made well."* Immediately the fountain of her blood was dried up, and she felt in her body that she was healed of the affliction.

Mark 7:31–35: Again, departing from the region of Tyre and Sidon, He came through the midst of the region of Decapolis to the Sea of Galilee. Then they brought to Him one who was deaf and had an impediment in his speech, and *they begged Him to put His hand on him.* And He took him aside from the multitude, and put His fingers in his ears, and He spat and touched his tongue. Then, looking up to heaven, He sighed, and said to him, "Ephphatha," that is, "Be opened." Immediately his ears were opened, and the impediment of his tongue was loosed, and he spoke plainly.

Mark 10:46–52: Now they came to Jericho. As He went out of Jericho with His disciples and a great multitude, blind Bartimaeus, the son of Timaeus, sat by the road begging. And when he heard that it was Jesus of Nazareth, *he began to cry out* and say, "Jesus, Son of David, have mercy on me!" Then many warned him to be quiet; but he cried out all the more, "Son of David, have mercy on me!" So Jesus stood still and commanded him to be called. Then they called the blind man, saying to him, "Be of good cheer. Rise, He is calling you." And *throwing aside his garment, he rose and came to Jesus.* So Jesus answered and said to him, "What do you want Me to do for you?" The blind man said to Him, "Rabboni, that I may receive my sight." Then Jesus said to him, "Go your way; *your faith has made you well.*" And immediately he received his sight and followed Jesus on the road.

Luke 7:1–10: Now when He concluded all His sayings in the hearing of the people, He entered Capernaum. And a certain centurion's servant, who was dear to him, was sick and ready to die. So when he heard about Jesus, he sent elders of the Jews to Him, pleading with Him to come and heal his servant. And when they came to Jesus, they begged Him earnestly, saying that the one for whom He should do this was deserving, "for he loves our nation, and has built us a synagogue." Then Jesus went with them. And when He was already not far from the house, the centurion sent friends to Him, saying to Him, "Lord, do not trouble Yourself, for I am not worthy that You should enter under my roof. Therefore, I did not even think myself worthy to come to You. *But say the word, and my servant will be healed.* For I also am a man placed under authority, having soldiers under me. And I say to one, 'Go,' and he goes; and to another, 'Come,' and he comes; and to my servant, 'Do this,' and he does it. When Jesus heard these things, He marveled at him, and turned around and said to the crowd that followed Him, "I say to you, I have not found such great faith, not even in Israel!" And those who were sent, returning to the house, found the servant well who had been sick.

Acts 3:1–11: Now Peter and John went up together to the temple at the hour of prayer, the ninth hour. And a certain man lame from his mother's womb was carried, whom they laid daily at the gate of the temple which is called

Beautiful, to ask alms from those who entered the temple; who, seeing Peter and John about to go into the temple, asked for alms. And fixing his eyes on him, with John, Peter said, "Look at us." So *he gave them his attention*, expecting to receive something from them. Then Peter said, "Silver and gold I do not have, but what I do have I give you: In the name of Jesus Christ of Nazareth, rise up and walk." And he took him by the right hand and lifted him up, and immediately his feet and ankle bones received strength. So he, leaping up, stood and walked and entered the temple with them—walking, leaping, and praising God. And all the people saw him walking and praising God. Then they knew that it was he who sat begging alms at the Beautiful Gate of the temple; and they were filled with wonder and amazement at what had happened to him.

The key to removing a beggarly mindset is to start with thinking about what we *do* have and what we *can* do. All the individuals above did what they could do—they used their knowledge, connections, and understanding to take both bold physical and spiritual action to receive from the kingdom. Some of the work was their own, and when they knew more was required, they made a *personal, selective, and expectant request* to the One who could and would answer. We can and should use every gift, talent, and means God has given us to bring what He's made possible for us into our lives, demonstrating a faithfulness of what we have already been given, while knowing that when and if a gap or lack occurs, the impossible is made possible through our relationship and inheritance available in and with Him by taking bold steps of faith.

We must pursue the full benefit of our design—as we were made "just a little lower than the angels" to take charge over issues of the earth. We are able to do great things by the works of our hands to care for the works of His hands Who created this world (Heb. 2:7). He equips us to do what He called us to do (Heb. 13:20–21) and then gives us access to everything He has through His abundant grace for everything else (Rom. 5:17). All that we need to be complete and to live out the fullness of our spiritual identity is just a bold act of faith away!

Reflection Questions

Do you tend to focus more on lack, gaps, and needs in your life than on your spiritual position and privileges available as a joint heir with Christ?

How can knowing more about your spiritual identity lead you to being stronger and bolder, even in times of need?

When you go to Christ with a request, is it

- personal (reflective of your relationship with Him)?
- selective (because you know He is the only one who can)?
- expectant (with a clear outcome based on scripture in mind)?

CHAPTER 4

WHY ARE YOU
ASKIN' AGAIN?

Royalty thinks differently. They have the luxury of the knowledge of who they are, what they have at their disposal, and how to use their influence. Because of this, they have a high expectation of a good result and a strong sense of control. As an heir, we need to think differently as well. In this chapter, we will continue to challenge beggarly elements in our mindset that no longer belong or are ineffective in the kingdom of God. We know that a beggar must ask for something from others who have no obligation to give, even if they have it.

As a reminder, a beggarly mindset has three conditions:

1. Lack of one's own personal possessions or ability to meet one's own needs.
2. The need to ask others, often unknown to us, for what is needed without confidence of receiving.
3. A life of focus on the needs of self, without the capacity to care for or share generously with others.

A beggar has few resources of their own, so they rely on soliciting from others until the request(s) has resulted in some form of gain or the beggar tires of asking. It is the *repetitive, unproductive asks* that we will now explore together. Whom we ask things for needs to be selective, out of our personal relationship with Christ, and with an expectancy of a good outcome. To expect to receive is not a matter of mere wishing or wanting. Expectation comes from knowing the One we are asking to supply our need *and* from knowing our rights and responsibilities when making the request. The more we know what scripture tells us about God's will and our responsibilities, the more confident and assured we can be that God will hear us and respond to fill the need in our lives and that He will "make us whole" as part of the on-going and eternal gift of salvation.

> *We keep asking for what we need when we have*
> *already given the right to receive.*

One of the most important aspects of heirship is an understanding of whom we are seeking assistance from. When we seek and ask from God, we are assured to find what is needed. Matthew 7:7–8 tells us that we should "ask and it will be given to you; seek and you will find; knock and the door will be opened to you. For everyone who asks receives; the one who seeks finds; and to the one who knocks, the door will be opened."

This provides a huge amount of assurance to us when we approach Father God about our inheritance. We should approach with full expectation, yet we also have to recall from Galatians 4:2 that we, as children, are subject to the appointment and apportionment of the Father as to what we receive and when we receive His blessings as His heirs. Thus, knowing the will of the Father is very important when we pray to obtain from His kingdom.

> 1 John 5:13–15: These things have I written unto you that believe on the name of the Son of God; that ye may know that ye have eternal life, and that ye may believe on the name of the Son of God. And *this is the confidence that we have in him, that, if we ask anything according to his will, he hears us*: And if we know that he hears us, whatsoever we ask, we know that we have the petitions that we desired of him.

John tells us the key to confidence is knowing that God hears us, but we also see throughout scripture that *God is listening for us to want and ask*

31

for things that line up with His will. After all, what good father spends time entertaining childish requests or is enticed by granting wishes he knows will bring ultimate harm to the child or convey something contrary to the family values and rules that he has so clearly established?

God is omnipotent. He is above. He is divine. Yet knowing the will of God is not an impossible task. While His thoughts and ways are not the same as ours (Isa. 55:8), He has graciously provided us with the ability to learn His will. We can read the Word of God, we can pray and seek to understand it, and we can commune with the Holy Spirit placed in us for the purpose of guiding, teaching, and leading us to His will.

> John 16:13: But when he, the Spirit of truth, comes, *he will guide you into all the truth. He will not speak on his own; he will speak only what he hears*, and he will tell you what is yet to come.

> Romans 8:25–27: But if we hope for what we do not yet have, we wait for it patiently. In the same way, the Spirit helps us in our weakness. We do not know what we ought to pray for, but the Spirit himself intercedes for us through wordless groans. And he who searches our hearts knows the mind of the Spirit, because *the Spirit intercedes for God's people in accordance with the will of God.*

It is important that we take the time to learn the will of God. This is how we know Him more and how our relationship with Him grows. If we are unsure of the specifics of God's will in a particular situation, we can seek for His provision based on what *He knows* we need. Jesus taught us that when he instructed the disciples on prayer.

> Matthew 6:5–13: And when you pray, do not be like the hypocrites, for they love to pray standing in the synagogues and on the street corners to be seen by others. Truly I tell you, they have received their reward in full. But when you pray, go into your room, close the door and pray to your Father, who is unseen. Then your Father, who

sees what is done in secret, will reward you. And when you pray, do not keep on babbling like pagans, for they think they will be heard because of their many words. Do not be like them, for *your Father knows what you need before you ask him.* This, then, is how you should pray. "Our Father in heaven, hallowed be your name, *your kingdom come, your will be done, on earth as it is in heaven.* Give us today our daily bread. And forgive us our debts, as we also have forgiven our debtors. And lead us not into temptation but deliver us from the evil one."

This prayer covers provision, forgiveness, strength, and protection. It opens the spiritual door to receiving what we need for the day and *releases the will of the Father in heaven to have an impact on our lives here on earth.* When we think of the lives we will be living in heaven, do we believe God will provide everything that we need every day? If so, can we then extend that trust for Him to choose what to provide for us daily here on earth as well, inviting Him to start the same care now that is already set aside for us in the future? 2 Peter 1:3 tells us that God has the divine power to give us "all things that pertain unto life and godliness" here on earth and that His interest is not just in our eternal future.

The Lord's Prayer was given as a model to help create the habit of *inviting God's will as the most important element of desire in our lives.* When we pray it, we are stating, "Father, I trust you to take care of me in the ways You believe to be best because You care for me (1 Pet. 5:7), You have good thoughts and plans for me (Jer. 29:11), and You have a good, acceptable, and perfect will (Rom. 12:2) for my life." Whom else should we completely trust to take care of us each day? If He cares more for us than the sparrows (Matt. 10:31) and has numbered the hairs on our heads (Luke 12:7), shouldn't we have a complete confidence that He will provide the best answer to addressing our needs if we come to Him, praising His name and asking that His will and His kingdom come into our lives? If so, we do not need to ask others what we should be asking Him for, and we should have a confidence that if what we ask for is of His will, He will hear it and provide it—because we are His children and heirs. Our parent-child relationship is important to building this trust. We have the opportunity to come to know His nature as our Abba, Father, through the spiritual connection He has granted us (Gal. 4:6). Because we are in the same family, because we are joint heirs with Christ, and because we care about the same things as the Father and Son, we should be aligned in the requests we take before Him.

> 1 Corinthians 2:12–14: Now we have received, not the spirit of the world, but the spirit which is of God; *that we might know the things that are freely given to us of God.* Which things also we speak, not in the words which man's wisdom teaches, but which the Holy Ghost teaches; comparing spiritual things with spiritual. But the natural man receives not the things of the Spirit of God: for they are foolishness unto him: neither can he know them, because they are spiritually discerned.

We must get to know our Father's will through His Word and the Spirit within us that freely shares knowledge with us. The Spirit also provides the immediate comfort of His nature, discernment of God's will, and partnership of strength and comfort while we wait to see the goodness of God, the answer to our prayer, come forward. The Spirit is our companion who can calm our nerves, uplift our hearts, and change our perspective, from the inside out, even if there is no other change in circumstances. The fruit or nature of the Spirit dwelling in us isn't transferred to us, but we get to experience it as we spend time with the Spirit, so our own mind, will, and emotions can be influenced by the Spirit to effectively "wait upon the Lord" with renewed strength (Isa. 40:31).

> Galatians 5:22–23: But the fruit of the Spirit is love, joy, peace, forbearance, kindness, goodness, faithfulness, gentleness and self-control.

Take advantage of the self-control, the kindness, the peace, and the joy of the Spirit, which can provide emotional stability and strength as we turn to God to seek, learn, and accept His will for our lives. The Word of God is full of promises God has given to His heirs. He inspired the authors of the Bible to write everything that our spiritual position and identity grant us. His will is crafted in terms of promises made to those who will claim them. A promise (GK: *epaggelia*) is an announcement and pledge providing divine assurance of good. When we find the promises described in the Word of God, we have found His will and His goodness for our lives!

When we are collecting on a promise, we aren't asking for something with an unknown outcome like a beggar would. In fact, in terms of a promise, a commitment has been made to give us something very real, upon us doing what is required or by us simply letting the granter know that we'd like the promise fulfilled. In the case of us as heirs, we have been given promises by our Father, who has the ability and will to give, because He has pledged what He will do. He has written it down and sealed it in our hearts with the Holy Spirit. Further, God *has to* provide what was promised, because He isn't a man that He should lie (Heb. 6:18). We also know that all things were made by and for Him, so there is no shortage in His capacity to fulfill every promise He has made.

> 2 Corinthians 1:20: For all the promises of God in him
> are yea, and in him Amen, unto the glory of God by us.

Just like Abraham, we are heirs to the promises of God, and we redeem those promises through faith. Faith is the payment made; it is *our part* to express our understanding and desire to receive. Confidence and assurance (which is faith) is the requirement to request the promise. We must have read and believed what the will of God has told us is available. We can all reflect on times we were told we could have something—an allowance, a promotion, an opportunity—if we did something first. That might have been weekly chores, successful completion of a project, or taking care of an elderly person. Those are promises with conditions. In these cases, we must do work or take action to receive. There are also promises made for specific circumstances—like an aunt or uncle that tells a teen, "If you are ever in trouble, you can call me anytime, and I will come get you anywhere, no questions asked." So, *it is important that we fully read all terms of the will so we know when and how the Father has established how He intends to deliver His promises to His heirs*. Too often, we are tempted to scan scriptures to find a promise but do not attend to the conditions or circumstances that relate to the promise. When we do that, it is like ignoring an age restriction or other requirements of maturity placed in a will that prohibit the release of the inheritance while expecting the promise to be given on demand.

As all promises are activated by faith, we need to do our part to know what the Word, the will of God, says to have confidence that it is part of the inheritance promised and whether there are terms associated with receiving it. Once we know the promise and conditions, our faith can be launched, backed by actions as bold as the situation. In fact, most of our favorite scriptures tell us about *our role* in accessing the blessings we desire. If we fulfill the requirement with understanding and an expectant faith, we can know that our Father will do as He has stated it is His will to do:

> John 8:31–32: Then said Jesus to those Jews which believed on him, *If ye continue (abide in) my word,* then are ye my disciples indeed; And ye shall know the truth, and the truth shall make you free.

> 1 John 1:8–9: If we say that we have no sin, we deceive ourselves, and the truth is not in us. *If we confess our sins,* he is faithful and just to forgive us our sins, and to cleanse us from all unrighteousness.

> Romans 8:28: And we know that all things work together for good to *them that love God, to them who are the called according to his purpose.*

> Psalm 37:3–5: *Trust in the Lord, and do good*; so shalt thou dwell in the land, and verily thou shalt be fed. *Delight thyself also in the Lord*: and he shall give thee the desires of thine heart. *Commit thy way* unto the Lord; *trust also in him*; and he shall bring it to pass.

We may ask God to reveal truth to us, but He has told us that a habit of reading and applying His Word in our lives will bring us that understanding. We need forgiveness from sin, which still comes so easy to our old nature, and He tells us that we simply need to confess those sins to Him to find it. We can be confident that everything will work out for our good *if* we keep our focus on loving Him and doing what He has created us to do. It is a lifetime investment to know Him and His will more, and everything we learn should increase how much we trust Him, delight in Him, and commit ourselves to follow Him. *As we focus on becoming mature heirs in the kingdom of God who passionately pursue His will, He is at liberty to issue more of the inheritance to us,* honoring not only our needs but our desires as well. The more we know Him, the more we will know His will and do the good He has called us to do, which positions us properly to receive what our Father has promised us to live and serve boldly, bringing ourselves security and Him glory. By being in alignment with His will, when we do ask, He will hear and provide.

Faith requires persistence, and that persistence requires action. Faith without works is dead. Therefore, faith isn't just "really believing that God will"; *faith is doing our part* with such an earnest heart that He sees it and registers it as a sign that we are ready for the apportionment of His promise. Our confidence has to translate to action that fulfills the conditions of the promises He has issued for us to receive—after all, He cannot lie, and He wrote down what we needed to know and do for the release of the promised blessing to come. In fact, even salvation, the free gift promised by God, required our belief and confession to be fulfilled in our lives (Rom. 10:9–10).

> James 2:17–18: Even so faith, if it hath not works, is dead, being alone. Yea, a man may say, Thou hast faith, and I have works: shew me thy faith without thy works, and I will shew thee my faith by my works.

There are many things God, our Father, has identified for us to be, have, possess, share in, abide in, hold, and obtain. We are a chosen generation, a royal priesthood, His own special people. Prior to becoming a joint heir, we were not His and we did not have access to these things. But now, in Christ, we have obtained mercy, forgiveness, and access to a supply of all things good and all things that are needed (1 Pet. 2:9–12); it is our choice *to believe and act* according to the spiritual identity of heirship that brings this abundance into our lives.

Our Father is asking us to know what is in His will, the Word of God, and then to enter negotiations with Him about it. Know that part of His will is His expectation that we do our part as much as we expect Him to fulfill the promises He has made to us. His promises are yes and amen. He is clear about them and prepared to fulfill them for everyone who activates them with faith. Yet we need to know which ones require us to do our part, as those will not be released by repeated requests to a Father, who likely shakes His head at His child, saying, "Child, didn't I already promise you that?" or "Didn't I tell you how to receive it?" or "If you do your part, will I not fulfill My Word and make you whole?" Many times, the faith required is an action and not a verbal request, and if we take the prerequisite action, knowing His promised response, we will release and enjoy the inheritance.

Everything in the Word is within the Father and Son's authority to deliver. They have the capacity to do the miraculous, the wonderful, and the mighty. Their thoughts, their ways, their will are important to seek as those are what we want to see introduced "in the land of the living" (Ps. 27:13) to change what already is into what could be. One of our first acts of faith is to expect our spiritual family of God, the Father, and Christ, our Brother, to know about, care about, and be ready to share in life with us here, today, as we learn about and live out His will. We should not only be confident in their love, authority, truth, and promises but also be prepared to do the works that He has called to be our demonstration of our faith and our responsibility to the family. It isn't always easy, but the Holy Spirit has been given to help make us able. As children of God, we must be willing to pick up our cross and follow our Lord (Mark 8:34–35) daily, to invest in growing up in the things of faith, to receive what He has established for us to have both here on earth and to build up our inheritance in heaven. If we learn, speak, and do as He has called us to do, the will of the Father will see us through!

Reflection Questions

What should you do to learn what God's will is before you ask Him for something?

Did you know that most promises of God included things for *you* to do to receive? Have you ever seen and focused on the conditions of the promises before?

How might you increase demonstration of your faith through works that prove your confidence in God's promises?

CHAPTER 5

You've Got Plenty to Share

The more we learn about our place in the kingdom of God, the further and further away we get from our definition of beggarly and the more we can challenge any ongoing thoughts of lack. We also come to realize that we have a responsibility as heirs; we have been given our position and abilities for a reason. We have to know our place in the kingdom and take bold steps of faith, doing what God has called us to do to receive the promises recorded in His will. We never need to fixate on unmet needs when we have strengths, abilities, access, provision, and assurances granted by our Father to address those needs in a myriad of ways that exceed what we currently see. If we are spending too much time in survival mode, we have drifted from our ability to be like our Father God—thoughtful, confident, generous, and concerned about the welfare of others.

A beggarly mindset has three conditions:

1. Lack of one's own personal possessions or ability to meet one's own needs.
2. The need to ask others, often unknown to us, for what is needed without confidence of receiving.
3. A life of focus on the needs of self, without the capacity to care for or share generously with others.

As we have worked through the first two elements of a beggarly condition, we can now turn to the last, recognizing that fixation on self diminishes our ability to see and care for others well. We were placed in this world, in our families, and in our spheres of influence, such as our workplace and community, to share our God-given talents and the love that resides in us with others. If we haven't let God care for us and supply our need, we will likely be unable to give of ourselves and our resources generously to others.

When you know how to make the fountain flow, you don't
have to worry about trying to make it pool at your feet.

God's heirs should have a heart of service and generosity that reflects His own. He has committed to supply our needs based on the riches He holds possession of in glory (Phil. 4:19). As He provides for us and as we understand how limitless and sustaining His promises are, we can let go of fear about tomorrow and focus on serving Him as best we can today. What we give on His behalf, He has the power to replace and to replenish in our lives. When God gives, He gives back "pressed down, shaken together and running over" (Luke 6:38), so the giving is always recognized, rewarded, and restored.

> Matthew 6:24–34: No one can serve two masters; for either he will hate the one and love the other, or else he will be loyal to the one and despise the other. You cannot serve God and mammon. Therefore, I say to you, *do not worry* about your life, what you will eat or what you will drink; nor about your body, what you will put on. Is not life more than food and the body more than clothing? Look at the birds of the air, for they neither sow nor reap nor gather into barns; yet your heavenly Father feeds them. Are you not of more value than they? Which of you by worrying can add one cubit to his stature? So why do you worry about clothing? Consider the lilies of the field, how they grow: they neither toil nor spin; and yet I say to you that even Solomon in all his glory was not arrayed like one of these. Now if God so clothes the grass of the field,

which today is, and tomorrow is thrown into the oven, will He not much more clothe you, O you of little faith? Therefore, *do not worry*, saying, "What shall we eat?" or "What shall we drink?" or "What shall we wear?" For after all these things the Gentiles seek. For your heavenly Father knows that you need all these things. *But seek first the kingdom of God and His righteousness, and all these things shall be added to you. Therefore, do not worry about tomorrow, for tomorrow will worry about its own things. Sufficient for the day is its own trouble.*

It's a privilege to think, "what can I do with what God has given me to help another?", compared to worrying about if and when our needs will be met. We must remember that God hasn't provided us with what we have to put us in bondage of the fear of losing it. There shouldn't be an overprotective or misery approach to hoarding what we have. When we open our hands to give, we are also well positioned to receive again.

Acts 20:35: I have shewed you all things, how that so laboring ye ought to support the weak, and to remember the words of the Lord Jesus, how he said, *It is more blessed to give than to receive.*

Our Father made us to be like Him, and our thinking should reflect this. We are to leave the weak and beggarly elements (fundamental principles or rudimentary beliefs) that we know God would never hold and replace them with thoughts of strength and abundance. We must embrace the knowledge that our spiritual identity makes us a giver of great things because we share in the family's wealth and generosity. We have been taught how to share by our Father; He has clearly expressed generosity as a value He wants us to demonstrate. Scripture abounds with the truth that our Father is a giver.

John 3:16: For God *so loved the world that he gave* his one and only Son, that whoever believes in him shall not perish but have eternal life.

James 1:16–17: Don't be deceived, my dear brothers and sisters. *Every good and perfect gift is from above, coming down from the Father* of the heavenly lights, who does not change like shifting shadows.

1 Corinthians 15:57: But thanks be to God! He gives us the victory through our Lord Jesus Christ.

1 Corinthians 2:12: What we have received is not the spirit of the world, but the Spirit who is from God, so that we may understand what God has freely given us.

John 14:27: Peace I leave with you, My peace I give to you; not as the world gives do I give to you. Let not your heart be troubled, neither let it be afraid.

Not only is God generous in giving out of His love for us, but He also establishes another promise with a condition for us to follow, making it clear that we set the pace for the generosity we experience in our lives based on how well we embrace our role as givers.

Luke 6:38: Give, and it shall be given unto you; good measure, pressed down, and shaken together, and running over, shall men give into your bosom. *For with the same measure that ye mete withal it shall be measured to you* again.

2 Corinthians 9:6–8: But this I say, *He which soweth sparingly shall reap also sparingly; and he which soweth bountifully shall reap also bountifully.* Every man according as he purposes in his heart, so let him give; not grudgingly, or of necessity: for God loveth a cheerful giver. And God is able to make all grace abound toward you; that ye, always having all sufficiency in all things, may abound to every good work.

Matthew 7:9–12: Which of you, if your son asks for bread, will give him a stone? Or if he asks for a fish, will give him a snake? If you, then, though you are evil, know how to give good gifts to your children, how much more will your Father in heaven give good gifts to those who ask him! *So in everything, do to others what you would have them do to you,* for this sums up the Law and the Prophets.

Giving is the foundation of a good relationship of trust. When we know that the supply never runs dry and when we know that all we have is because of the will and promises of the Father in our lives, we are able to let riches *pass through us* to benefit everyone around us. When our Father trusts us to use what He has given us graciously and wisely, He then can offer more. Just as every parent wants to care for their child, they also do not want their child to be wasteful, spoiled, and ungrateful for what they have. This is part of the reason God has retained His ability to apportion the inheritance in alignment with our maturity. In fact, God established a way of charging us to show our understanding of His provision and our recognition of our need to invest what we have for His kingdom and glory. God established the practice of tithing early in His relationship with man, noting that a portion of what God gives (10 percent) is to be directed into His kingdom, allowing for the remaining 90 percent to be used to meet one's own needs and to make an impact on the world:

Genesis 28:22: Then Jacob made a vow, saying, "If God will be with me and will watch over me on this journey I am taking and will give me food to eat and clothes to wear so that I return safely to my father's household, then the Lord will be my God and this stone that I have set up as a pillar will be God's house, and of all that you give me I will give you a tenth."

Malachi 3:7–11: "Ever since the time of your ancestors you have turned away from my decrees and have not kept them. Return to me, and I will return to you," says the Lord Almighty. "But you ask, 'How are we to return?'

Will a mere mortal rob God? Yet you rob me. But you ask, 'How are we robbing you?' In tithes and offerings. You are under a curse—your whole nation—because you are robbing me. Bring the whole tithe into the storehouse, that there may be food in my house. Test me in this," says the Lord Almighty, "and see if I will not throw open the floodgates of heaven and pour out so much blessing that there will not be room enough to store it. I will prevent pests from devouring your crops, and the vines in your fields will not drop their fruit before it is ripe," says the Lord Almighty.

Giving is an outpouring of a heart condition. When we give, we are doing what our Father has taught us to do. It is an act of both obedience and trust. Throughout scripture, we are encouraged to be a lender and not a borrower (Prov. 22:7). We are not to be one who takes but does not repay; the righteous are those who give generously because we recognize the unmerited favor that has been freely poured out on our lives (Ps. 37:21). We are given more than we have earned or deserve, so we shouldn't bind others to only what they have earned or deserve as well. When we think of all we have received—forgiveness, love, provision, righteousness—we have to acknowledge that we have much to give and an obligation to pay it forward. Often, we have the most to offer others in the areas where we once struggled and God met our needs. This has led to a perspective and a testimony, and God positions us to do the same for another both directly through offering our wisdom and service and through our introducing Him to those who now reside where we once have been. *Freely you have received, so freely you must give* (Matt. 10:9)—another family value God expects us to embrace and live by. In fact, God tells us, when we take the time to take care for others, He views it as us doing something for Him, and He will provide eternal rewards to us based on how we used what He gave us to make life better for others.

Matthew 25:34–40: Then the King will say to those on His right hand, "Come, you blessed of My Father, inherit the kingdom prepared for you from the foundation of the world: for I was hungry and you gave Me food; I was thirsty and you gave Me drink; I was a stranger and you took Me in; I was naked and you clothed Me; I was sick and you visited Me; I was in prison and you came to Me." Then the righteous will answer Him, saying, "Lord, when did we see You hungry and feed You, or thirsty and give You drink? When did we see You a stranger and take You in, or naked and clothe You? Or when did we see You sick, or in prison, and come to You?" And the King will answer and say to them, "Assuredly, I say to you, inasmuch as you did it to one of the least of these My brethren, you did it to Me."

Giving is more than extending money; we must give our hearts and minds to be changed. David "gave himself in prayer" to get ready to serve God well (Ps. 109:4) so he could stand firm within the situation before him. When selecting leaders in the young church, God commanded that they look for individuals "of good reputation, full of the Holy Spirit and wisdom" who could be appointed over the ministry's work and who could give themselves to ministering the Word (Acts 6:3–4). Peter and John went about God's business, offering what they could—aiding a man by proclaiming, "In the Name of Jesus Christ of Nazareth, stand up and walk!" (Acts 3:6). We can sometimes shirk our own call or opportunities to give, noting that we are not a Paul, a Peter, an apostle, or a pastor, yet we are all still His children, positioned in heavenly places and made in His image and for a distinctive fearful and marvelous purpose. Our design will be revealed in us the more we *give ourselves* to the life God has called us to live. When He nudges us to give wisdom, a word of encouragement, a car ride, a kindness—anything the Spirit in us wants extended to the person beside us—get used to saying, "Yes, Lord." The more we do, the more we are like Christ, our Brother, who did the Father's will "upon impulse" and by the Spirit's unction, and by doing so, showed the world God's unconditional love in the most meaningful ways.

John 5:19–21: Then Jesus answered and said to them, "Most assuredly, I say to you, the Son can do nothing of

Himself, but what He sees the Father do; for whatever He does, the Son also does in like manner. For the Father loves the Son and shows Him all things that He Himself does; and He will show Him greater works than these, that you may marvel. For as the Father raises the dead and gives life to them, even so the Son gives life to whom He will."

1 Timothy 4:12–16: Let no one despise your youth, but be an example to the believers in word, in conduct, in love, in spirit, in faith, in purity. Till I come, give attention to reading, to exhortation, to doctrine. *Do not neglect the gift that is in you*, which was given to you by prophecy with the laying on of the hands of the eldership. *Meditate on these things; give yourself entirely to them, that your progress may be evident to all.* Take heed to yourself and to the doctrine. Continue in them, for in doing this you will save both yourself and those who hear you.

Romans 12:3–8: For I say, through the grace given to me, to everyone who is among you, not to think of himself more highly than he ought to think, but to think soberly, as God has dealt to each one a measure of faith. For as we have many members in one body, but all the members do not have the same function, so we, being many, are one body in Christ, and individually members of one another. *Having then gifts differing according to the grace that is given to us, let us use them*: if prophecy, let us prophesy in proportion to our faith; or ministry, let us use it in our ministering; he who teaches, in teaching; he who exhorts, in exhortation; he who gives, with liberality; he who leads, with diligence; he who shows mercy, with cheerfulness.

Remember that giving is part of our spiritual nature once we are in God's family. Giving is the conduit for God's provision and wellness to reach a lost and dying world. We are His children and His ambassadors, and we must give time, talents, and treasures bestowed upon us liberally for people to realize that the God enabling us to give is real, loving, and kind. How else are they to come to know Him if not through us? The goodness of God should be evident as we give of ourselves as the redeemed, restored, equipped, mature, and confident children of a loving Father. It is about giving not only money and service but also the love and kindness within us. God showed that He valued time and relationship as much as service through Christ's message to Mary and Martha (Luke 10:38–42). In fact, God applauded the woman who did a great thing by anointing His feet with oil, while the disciples focused on what could have been bought with the money (Mark 14:3–6). The message: yes, give out of the abundance of wealth God may put in our hands to have, but don't start and stop there. Embrace who we are, the wisdom we have gained, the love in our hearts, and sit and share it with the people who don't have any other conduit for receiving the goodness of God in their lives.

When we focus on "our lives" and "our needs," we miss out on being the pipeline for others to receive their blessing from God through us. When we can be content with what we have and hold an expectation that it will always be more than enough, then God knows that we are ready to give what we have away and can be entrusted with more.

> 1 Timothy 6:7–9: For we brought nothing into this world, and it is certain we can carry nothing out. *And having food and clothing, with these we shall be content.* But those who desire to be rich fall into temptation and a snare, and into many foolish and harmful lusts which drown men in destruction and perdition.

> 1 Timothy 6:17–19: Command those who are rich in this present age not to be haughty, *nor to trust in uncertain riches but in the living God, who gives us richly all things to enjoy.* Let them do good, that they be rich in good works, ready to give, willing to share, storing up for themselves a good foundation for the time to come, that they may lay hold on eternal life.

Whatever we have—time, knowledge, resources, and abilities—has been given to us to meet our own needs *and* for us to share with others. When we focus on receiving from the Father so we can do His will and give to others, we will find that He increases what is entrusted to us, and we will never experience lack because we will have made ourselves a pipeline of His goodness and glory.

Reflection Questions

Have you ever felt fearful to give because you thought you didn't have enough for your own needs? If so, how did you overcome that? If that is a current concern, how can you address the fear of lack and become a giver of 10 percent?

What opportunities did God give you to share your time, talents, or treasure generously in the last year? How did you respond?

CHAPTER 6

MY WILL, MY LIFE

There is long-standing and unfortunate history of slavery in our world that provides us with a real-life example of the pain and depravity of bondage—of persons forced to work for and obey another, of persons considered the property of another, and of those stripped of voice and power. It is particularly harmful in that it quenches the gift of the will that God gave to humankind, His favorite creation. And while we may feel like this practice is well behind us, its roots are deep in the lasting influence that bondage creates in the human psyche as well as the diminished opportunities and possibilities that linger well beyond emancipation. This type of experience not only wears on the slave physically and mentally but also changes the rights and privileges of the generations to follow. It erodes conviction that self-determination matters when the quality of one's life is completely subject to the will of the owner. From this dark earthly example, we can see the deep contrast with God's kingdom. He did not make us slaves; He invited us to be heirs. He has wealth and power to share, and He wants His descendants to have an advantage through every generation. He hasn't stripped us of our will or voice, but He invites us to use them freely and rightly to determine the quality of our lives and the legacy we will leave.

Conversely to a slave, a servant (GK: *diakonos*) is one who performs duties for others, with or without compensation, taking the position of a personal attendant. The interest of the servant is the care and well-being of whom they serve. *The will of the servant determines the services they will give, whereas it is only the will of the master who determines the service of the slave.* While the giving may look the same, the inherent difference between slave and servant is *choice.* If we are willingly giving ourselves up for another, we are serving and sacrificing for a relationship and a cause. If we are trapped in servitude, then we are in bondage, a slave to something or someone whom we cannot challenge or confront and in a situation that cannot be changed without great cost or loss. Anytime we feel our will is limited, we must pause and consider—Are we living as servant or slave? Have we chosen to surrender or has our power been taken? Confronting these questions helps us recognize situations when we may be acting as agents in bondage instead of agents of service. It will help us determine if we have surrendered our will unnecessarily, accepting bonds and residing in a position that returns us to a place that God sacrificed His Son to free us from.

> Galatians 4:1–9: Now I say, That the heir, as long as he is a child, differs nothing from a servant, though he be lord of all; But is under tutors and governors until the time appointed of the father. *Even so we, when we were children, were in bondage under the elements of the world:* But when the fulness of the time was come, God sent forth his Son, made of a woman, made under the law, to redeem them that were under the law, that we might receive the adoption of sons. And because ye are sons, God hath sent forth the Spirit of his Son into your hearts, crying, Abba, Father. Wherefore thou art no more a servant, but a son; and if a son, then an heir of God through Christ. *Howbeit then, when ye knew not God, ye did service unto them which by nature are no gods.* But now, after that ye have known God, or rather are known of God, how turn ye again to the weak and beggarly elements, whereunto *ye desire again to be in bondage?*

If we remain young in our thinking, as babes in the faith, we can remain bound to the way the world wants us to think about ourselves— dictating what we cannot do or what we think we have to do. It can convince us that we have no power or control to change our lives or to stand against the influence of life's situations. Being bound to the elements of the world takes away our conviction that we can be as God has made and called us to be—powerful, effective, and influential. The enemy would want to enslave us with shame, guilt, and victim-thinking, all at the cost of making us less able to serve the kingdom of God.

Being a slave in bondage creates three conditions:

1. A slave does not have a lasting position in the household one serves, nor does one's will matter to the master.
2. A slave hasn't chosen one's master, like a servant chooses whom they serve.
3. A mindset of slavery stays and invites ongoing bondage and submission to things one believes one cannot control.

Each of these conditions is held in place by a mindset and belief system that convinces the slave that change is impossible and that resistance is futile. If we don't realize our position in the household of God and our relationship to our Master, we can diminish our voice and fail to assert the power God gave us to be self-determined in choosing each day whom we will serve and the quality of life we have been called to live.

*Our sense of power comes from the position we
take and the perspectives we hold.*

We have already established that we are joint heirs with Christ granted rights, possessions, and a position in the kingdom of God. We are part of the ruling class, not slaves bound and controlled by others. This revelation forms the seed of knowledge that *we have the power of choice over whom we yield ourselves to.* We choose when to submit and when to sacrifice, serve, and surrender. These are choices that God has given us, which no manner of humanity can take away. It is a gift that comes from the free will He placed in us. Our design is to have the power of choice, often with the foreknowledge of the consequences of those choices. *We are self-determined beings, and if we embrace that, we will set our minds to obtain the life He's promised us.* Free will is our God-given ability to freely choose for ourselves. We see this privilege from the first moment in the Garden of Eden (Gen.

3), when Adam and Eve were allowed to choose whether to eat from the tree of knowledge. And we also see that their choice led to judgment, as it is only fair for God to judge us if there was a real choice available to be made. Often, we want to focus on the serpent's power to deceive, but God first makes it known that *we have the power to decide* whom we will listen to and whom we will honor.

That power opens the door to many good and wonderful things for us, not just bad consequences for choosing poorly. In fact, one of the greatest gifts of our inheritance is that God has provided redemption for our bad choices. He justifies us and makes us righteous, covering our sin and err, and opens the pathway for us to choose *differently* from what the world offers. His redemption comes to us through a choice to believe and confess (Rom. 10:9–10). He offers salvation freely, but we must be a "whosoever" that believes to receive everlasting life (John 3:16). And the gifts and rights that come through choice don't end at the cross. While direction, love, and power continuously flow from our Father, we must choose to receive from Him and to seek and serve Him daily to receive the benefits. We must be listening to hear His voice. We must open our hearts to embrace the love He gives. We must walk in the power bestowed upon us to bring its impact into our lives. He hasn't created robots who must do what He says. We hold the keys to receiving our inheritance and spiritual blessings, because we must choose to believe His promises, which includes embracing the liberty He gives us to be free from elements that would enslave us. When we joined God's kingdom, we became the complete opposite of a slave because:

- We can possess things that belong to the family.
- We have shared authority with other family members.
- We have a voice that is heard and are granted opportunities that are only shared within the family.
- We can choose to obey (or not) with consequences of, but not unbridled punishment for, disobedience.

Because God has brought us into the family through the free will of our choice to repent and receive, our mindset should not be that any aspect of our lives, spiritual or natural, is out of our control or forced upon us. We chose God. We chose grace, and we can continue to choose the benefits of our familial rank in His kingdom each day. As we use our will to do the things of the kingdom, we become more and more acknowledged by Christ as brethren (Mark 3:35).

> 1 John 3:1–3: Behold, *what manner of love the Father hath bestowed upon us*, that we should be called the sons of God: therefore, the world knows us not, because it knew him not. Beloved, now are we the sons of God, and it doth not yet appear what we shall be: but we know that, when he shall appear, we shall be like him; for we shall see him as he is. And every man that hath this hope in him purifies himself, even as he is pure.

> Hebrews 2:9–11: But we see Jesus, who was made a little lower than the angels for the suffering of death, crowned with glory and honor; that he by the grace of God should taste death for every man. For it became him, *for whom are all things, and by whom are all things, in bringing many sons unto glory*, to make the captain of their salvation perfect through sufferings. For both he that sanctifies, and they who are sanctified are all of one: for which cause *he is not ashamed to call them brethren.*

> Colossians 1:12–14: Giving thanks unto the Father, which hath made us meet to be *partakers of the inheritance* of the saints in light: Who hath *delivered us from the power of darkness*, and hath translated us into the kingdom of his dear Son: In whom we have redemption through his blood, even the forgiveness of sins.

There is a spiritual authority and influence that comes from being God's child. He has delivered us from the power of darkness. He has made it so we are not *subject* to it. When we are subject (GK: *hupotasso*) to something or someone, we are subordinate to them; we must obey and are under an obligation to submit ourselves under their rule. The word *subject* provides us with a visual description of being subdued, tied up, and held bound. There are many elements of this world that intend to ensnare us; in fact, the enemy has a great desire to take us captive so that we serve his will (2 Tim. 2:26), yet, through Christ, we are not bound to darkness, evil, or the elements of this world designed to cause harm and pain. We are no longer made to walk according to the elements of this world or in response to the prince of the power of the air (Eph. 2:2) because we have a new Lord and a new Father, who freed us from the hold of the enemy and made us a new creation. As children of God, we are *subject* to the consequences of our choices but *freed* from the condemnation (Rom. 8:1), the punishment (Matt. 25:46), and the wrath (1 Thess. 5:9) of an unforgiving and merciless master who can take unbridled anger out upon a slave. Our position is one of freedom, to think and do what our will inspires us to do, so our mindset and perspective should always be focused on our abilities and freedoms - and how we use them.

Influences will come at us from all directions, but they will fall into two buckets of servitude: one master attempting to control us and one offering us the opportunity to serve Him. From early on, God made it clear to Israel that multiple "gods" and "idols" would exist and that they would need to identify the One True Living God and decide whom they would follow and serve. Joshua took that question to the people, "Choose you this day whom ye will serve; whether the gods which your fathers served that were on the other side of the flood, or the gods of the Amorites, in whose land ye dwell: but as for me and my house, we will serve the Lord" (Josh. 24:15). *We use our will to choose each day what we will allow ourselves to be subject to and what and whom we will submit to.* That is the privilege, responsibility, and power God has given us by making us like Him (Gen. 1:27); an amazing creation with a soul and spirit, and with sovereignty of choice. If we use our will to align with Him, His will is established to fulfill His promises to us in return.

> John 14:23: Jesus answered and said unto him, if a man love me, he will keep my words: and my Father will love him, and we will come unto him, and make our abode with him.

Our Creator and Father God charges us to think like He does—as one without fear, as one that wisely uses the powerful will within. We are equipped to be intentional and thoughtful about how we choose to view ourselves, others, and the situation at hand. We are not controlled by the ways of the world and are not to be conditioned or enslaved to live *reactively* in response to it. We are to live boldly, representatively of the kingdom. This means we aren't restricted by the forces or influences upon or within us without the ability to choose to submit or resist (James 4:7) them. Either choice (submission or resistance) becomes an act of service to either the one intending to deceive or control us, or the one requesting that we learn, grow, obey, and serve Him. The more we "own" our power of choice, the more independent and self-determined we will look and feel, even to ourselves. The more we embrace this power within us, the more we will use our will to influence change and take charge of the life He's given us to live. As we live less reactively in response to demands and influences of the world, we become more peculiar (1 Pet. 2:9), standing out as people who do not conform to the patterns of this world (Rom. 12:2), who are less and less restricted by the confines of how the world operates. We have less fear, we hold less hurt, we release our insecurities, and our confidence and boldness in doing good in God's eyes soars. Once we embrace our right, privilege, and responsibility to choose well, we can better control our minds, will, and emotions in service to our Lord and our Father God.

> Romans 8:15–22: For ye have *not received the spirit of bondage again to fear*; but ye have received the Spirit of adoption, whereby we cry, Abba, Father. The Spirit itself bears witness with our spirit, that we are the children of God: And if children, then heirs; heirs of God, and joint-heirs with Christ; if so be that we suffer with him, that we may be also glorified together. For I reckon that the sufferings of this present time are not worthy to be compared with the glory which shall be revealed in us. For the earnest expectation of the creature waits for the manifestation of the sons of God. For the creature (creation) was made subject to vanity, not willingly, but by reason of him who hath subjected the same in hope,

Because the creature (creation) itself also *shall be delivered from the bondage of corruption into the glorious liberty of the children of God*. For we know that the whole creation groans and travails in pain together until now.

Note that the creature or all of God's creation is waiting for us, those who have the light and who are heirs of God's promise, and who will not be held down by fear, pain, or darkness, to bring the abundance of heaven down into this world. *The world needs to be influenced by God's children and heirs, not the other way around.* Whom and what we choose to obey and serve should come as a direct reflection of our choice to be in service to what God, the Father, has taught us and shared with us. We are in this world but not controlled by it. While we must respond to situations and circumstances each day, we should always do so in a thoughtful way without giving problems a position of power over our individual thoughts and choices. We can deal with natural problems with good, practical solutions from the perspective of knowing that there is also a spiritual response available to us that brings life and liberty to every situation. When challenged, scared, or confused, we have a direct line to the Father, who knows our needs and interests and has stated in His Word that they matter to Him. We have been given a voice before His throne and have been invited to engage our family, our Father, our Master, and friend in navigating and negotiating change. We are to be self-determined to both *will and do* what God has put us into position to do, which those who do not know Him, cannot.

Philippians 2:12–15: Wherefore, my beloved, as ye have always obeyed, not as in my presence only, but now much more in my absence, work out your own salvation with fear and trembling. *For it is God which worketh in you both to will and to do of his good pleasure.* Do all things without murmurings and disputing: That ye may be blameless and harmless, the sons of God, without rebuke, in the midst of a crooked and perverse nation, among whom ye shine as lights in the world.

Titus 3:1–9: Put them in mind to be subject to principalities and powers, to obey magistrates, to be ready to every good work, to speak evil of no man, to be no brawlers, but gentle, shewing all meekness unto all men. For we ourselves also were sometimes foolish, disobedient, deceived, serving divers lusts and pleasures, living in malice and envy, hateful, and hating one another. But after that the kindness and love of God our Savior toward man appeared, *Not by works of righteousness which we have done, but according to his mercy he saved us, by the washing of regeneration, and renewing of the Holy Ghost*; Which he shed on us abundantly through Jesus Christ our Savior. That being justified by his grace, we should be made heirs according to the hope of eternal life. This is a faithful saying, *and these things I will that thou affirm constantly, that they which have believed in God might be careful to maintain good works.* These things are good and profitable unto men. But avoid foolish questions, and genealogies, and contentions, and strivings about the law; for they are unprofitable and vain.

Sometimes, we read scripture and feel bondage about "not being good enough." Scripture tells us the goals God has for our transformation, and we are given a charge to grow spiritually; however, He is also clear that this work cannot be accomplished alone. We grow and serve Him well because of the regeneration of our spirit and partnership with the Holy Spirit. Our spiritual position enables us to do good in spite of the bad others do, to be meek when we recognize short fallings in others. We should realize that we were once children of wrath as well (Eph. 2:2–3) who used to allow desires, fears, and doubts to control us. Our own thoughts and opinions would rule us because we allowed them to and knew no better. We were totally subjected to and subdued by our old nature; but no more. *Because of the grace God has given, we are able to affirm constantly that we are the difference the world needs to see.* We can now know, believe, and *set our will* to the conviction that we can walk a different path from what the world offers; we can respond spiritually, engage our enemies differently, perceive with spiritual senses, and intentionally choose whom we will honor each day with our actions— Will it be God, our Father, and Christ, our Lord, or the prince of the powers of the air?

With our power of choice and self-determination (the process by which one controls their own life), we are equipped to continually resist the influence of the enemy and choose to submit to God and His ways and truth (James 4:7). We do this by examining every thought to determine whom it honors and which direction it would take us. Notice that this is an active, intentional choice, one which God has given us the power and responsibility to make. *We are our own masters because we have free will, and, therefore, the choice whether to serve another is our own.* The enemy wants to enslave us with self-centered thinking, yet God wants us to choose Him and to serve of our own volition. We see the way the enemy thinks and wants us to think from his attempt to overtake heaven.

> Isaiah 14:12–15: How art thou fallen from heaven, O Lucifer, son of the morning! how art thou cut down to the ground, which didst weaken the nations! For thou hast said in thine heart, I will ascend into heaven, I will exalt my throne above the stars of God: I will sit also upon the mount of the congregation, in the sides of the north: I will ascend above the heights of the clouds; I will be like the Most High. Yet thou shalt be brought down to hell, to the sides of the pit.

The enemy's two greatest tools are arrogance and deception; he loves to inspire both in us; however, we are not enslaved to accept or dwell in either perspective. They are not part of the spiritual identity we have been given. One of the greatest powers of our will is our ability to determine if and when we will yield. We determine what we will believe, what we will stand for, what we will do, what we won't do, when we will rise up and fight, and when we will lie down. We have authority to determine what we will give to another and what we won't. We have the ability to choose to tell the truth or to lie. We can humble ourselves and admit we are wrong or hold on to our opinions until they go with us to the grave, causing division along the way. We were made as independent beings with a charge to have dominion over the world (Gen. 1:26–28), over sin (Rom. 6:14), and over ourselves—*all possible* through wise use of our free will and our power of choice.

> Psalm 8:4–6: What is man, that thou art mindful of him? and the son of man, that thou visit him? For thou hast made him a little lower than the angels, and hast crowned him with glory and honor. Thou made him to have dominion over the works of thy hands; thou hast put all things under his feet.

> Colossians 1:15–16: Who is the image of the invisible God, the firstborn of every creature: For by him were all things created, that are in heaven, and that are in earth, visible and invisible, whether they be thrones, or dominions, or principalities, or powers: all things were created by him, and for him.

We were made with amazing capacity for self-determination and power, just like Christ, God's first begotten Son, and are charged with deciding how we will use our will and whom it will benefit. If we were created by and for a loving God, who brought us into His family, our will should follow a mindset of sonship, and sons, like servants, are asked to be obedient to the Father and head of house. *This obedience is not forced but is out of love and with an understanding of the well-stated consequences and rewards of service.* We know that the willing and obedient in God's kingdom eat the good of the land (Isa. 1:19). We know that obedience puts us on the pathway to receiving the inheritance of the promises in His will, as so many promises are contingent on us doing our part (if you do) to release His part (then I will). When we aren't obedient, those benefits and privileges remain unactualized, promises left unfulfilled because we refused to do our part, which is a matter of our will. The consequences of disobedience are meant to teach; they are meant to *reveal that the power of choice is in our hands* and is real. When we recognize how much power we have, we are less likely to believe that the enemy or this world has control over our destiny, and we become much more conscious of how we use the gift of our free will to not only receive salvation but also find victory, freedom, and wholeness.

It is our inherent right and responsibility to choose that relieves us from being a slave to the world, and in our choosing, we also exercise our right to determine whom we will serve. The Son Himself lived for one thing only, and that was to align His will to the will of the Father. That was how He used His power of choice.

> 1 John 5:1–4: Whosoever believeth that Jesus is the Christ is born of God: and everyone that loveth him that begat loveth him also that is begotten of him. By this we know that we love the children of God, when we love God, and keep his commandments. For this is the love of God, that we keep his commandments: and his commandments are not grievous. For whatsoever is born of God overcomes the world: and this is the victory that overcomes the world, even our faith.

> Hebrews 5:8–9: Though he were a Son, yet learned he obedience by the things which he suffered; and being made perfect, he became the author of eternal salvation unto all them that obey him.

> John 5:30: I can of mine own self do nothing: as I hear, I judge and my judgment is just; because I seek not mine own will, but the will of the Father which hath sent me.

> Matthew 12:49–50: And he stretched forth his hand toward his disciples, and said, Behold my mother and my brethren! For whosoever shall do the will of my Father which is in heaven, the same is my brother, and sister, and mother.

God provides not only chastisement, discipline, and correction for His children but also advice, guidance, support, fellowship, and reward to help guide our choices. Our will always remains active and empowered to respond to the opportunities given. God empowers us to use our will in wonderful ways—to love, forgive, endure, heal, overcome, and live in His abundance. Anything that quenches our sense of self-determination and tries to bind us, hold us hostage, or take away our voice and power is a reflection of slavery, and we must challenge its existence in our thought process. We can choose to be slaves to self—seeking to meet only our own desires or interests—but in doing so, we shift ourselves away from receiving the inheritance that comes from the choice of choosing to use our will to serve God's will. Our will is strong; it is what sets our hearts and minds on living in liberty and standing fast against any form of bondage. It is where our strength and resiliency are meant to come from. It determines the life we set our minds to have. If our will didn't matter and wasn't so crucial to our receiving the inheritance, there wouldn't be such a need to manage it and such rewards reserved for the choices we make with it!

Reflection Questions

Do you ever feel like life is "out of control"? How do you respond in those moments to regain a sense of God-given power and control?

How do you or can you use your will to be more intentional about how you live your life and whom you serve with it?

CHOOSING MY MASTER

Make no mistake, we have been purchased. We are owned. God has a right to call or consider us a possession, with no rights, privileges, or position in the kingdom, but He doesn't. He could have claimed us as slaves, but He didn't. He adopted us into the kingdom as sons and daughters; He Himself paying the ultimate placement fee to give us our familial rank.

> 1 Corinthians 6:19–20: What? know ye not that your body is the temple of the Holy Ghost which is in you, which ye have of God, and ye are not your own? For ye are bought with a price; therefore, glorify God in your body, and in your spirit, which are God's.

> 1 Corinthians 7:23: Ye are bought with a price; be not ye the servants of men.

As one bought with a price, it's important that we recognize what the cost of our adoption was. We are children of Deity and are now confronted with a decision on how we will respond to this privilege. Do we come into this new household with an awareness, humility, and desire to receive and honor not only the love of God but also His patriarchal authority over all? Do we yield to Him and choose to serve Him and the kingdom we have been adopted into? Or do we yearn for old ways and old things and resist coming into communion with Him and with our brothers and sisters in Christ? We have been purchased, redeemed, translated, sanctified; we are purged from being in bondage to sin, dead works, and our earthly heritage. We are empowered to serve the living God and receive the eternal inheritance. As adopted children, we are called to choose the role we will play in the family and to decide how connected with, and committed to, our spiritual kin we will be, much as with our physical family. We choose to speak proudly of our new heritage, or not. We choose to dive into deeper relationships with our brothers and sisters, or not. We decide how strong a representative of the kingdom we will be and are in the driver's seat when it comes to determining the life we will ultimately live. We either purge ourselves of the old things or dwell in them. We either embrace and pursue the promises of God or remain stagnant in our ways without the will to take action to receive more of what He has made possible and available to us. *Our destiny is ours to create based on the actions we are willing to take to fulfill it.*

> Hebrews 9:13–15: For if the blood of bulls and of goats, and the ashes of a heifer sprinkling the unclean, sanctifies to the purifying of the flesh, how much more shall the blood of Christ, who through the eternal Spirit offered himself without spot to God, *purge your conscience from dead works to serve the living God?* And for this cause he is the mediator of the new testament, that by means of death, for the redemption of the transgressions that were under the first testament, they which are called might *receive the promise of eternal inheritance.*

Therefore, we simply must choose to accept our place in the kingdom of God (Rom. 10:9–10) and determine if we will take the place and position of influence He has graciously offered us. Will we continue in old things and old ways, or will our conscience be cleansed to allow us to serve God with our whole heart and to live in the inheritance that has been promised? We choose whom we will serve with our lives and once that choice is made, it ultimately establishes the *quality of our lives* and *our destiny.*

Being a slave in bondage creates three conditions:

1. A slave does not have a lasting position in the household one serves, nor does one's will matter to the master.
2. A slave hasn't chosen one's master, like servants choose whom they serve.
3. A mindset of slavery stays and invites ongoing bondage and submission to things one believes one cannot control.

*Servants may choose their master, including the
quality, type, and term of service.*

We know that the children of Israel were God's chosen people by lineage and birthright and not by the spiritual rebirth of grace we experience today. While born into their heritage and inheritance, they still had to choose whether they were going to serve the God of their forefathers as a way of living or not. Even knowing their heritage gave them rights, they had to *choose whom they would serve* and, in doing so, established their Master and their pathway to receiving the inheritance.

> Joshua 24:15: And if it seems evil unto you to serve the Lord, *choose you this day whom ye will serve*; whether the gods which your fathers served that were on the other side of the flood, or the gods of the Amorites, in whose land ye dwell: but as for me and my house, we will serve the Lord.

Throughout the Old Testament, heroes of faith emerged. While their lineage (who begat who) was often outlined for us in scripture, it was not their lineage alone that mattered. They needed to be more than counted as descendants. Their life experience and inheritance were also contingent on their choice to serve God. There were even "non-Jews" like Rahab (Josh. 2:6; Heb. 11:31) who were honored because they made a choice to be "counted in" with God's people. They recognized that a birthright and bloodline existed that they wanted to be part of. They knew and believed in the heritage and inheritance offered by Israel's God, perhaps even more than some of the Israelites did. While we don't condone lying, cheating, and stealing as moral acts, we must recognize that God gave Jacob the birthright he stole from Esau (Gen. 27) and that Rahab lied to her own people to achieve her position of honor with God's people. Only Ruth simply said, "Your people will be my people, and your God will be my God" (Ruth 1:16) and pledged a loyalty that made her part of the bloodline of Christ—and an heir unto the promise. The bulk of the Old Testament is teaching us about the inheritance God has for His people *and* His desire for them to choose to live within it and serve Him faithfully to receive the benefits of it. That message can speak to our hearts today as we, too, determine "whom we will serve." Choosing a Lord and Master is a crucial element of our spiritual identity because it pulls us beyond the boundaries of self and gives us a place in a kingdom that has deep meaning, a powerful cause, and eternal impacts. God is an advantageous choice as Master, as He is a rewarder of those who diligently seek Him (Heb. 11:6).

There are many examples of service performed by one to receive a reward. In Genesis 29, we read how Jacob worked seven years for both Rachel and Leah to be his wives. He made that choice to serve, which is different from the forced servitude of slavery. Jacob shared a familial relationship and held on to the promise of what he would receive, which made him willingly submit to Laban as his master. We, now as children of God, confess Jesus as Lord of our lives in exchange for the gift of His redemption of our lives. We agree to the transaction, fully aware of the benefits to ourselves and acknowledging the nature of the one whom we will call Master. Christ came to give us a liberty of consciousness—the ability to make our own choice and have our own direct relationship with God without any barriers or other intermediary. He doesn't enslave us or force us to call Him Lord. We are fully able to choose and accept the consequence of the choice of whom we live in service to.

> Romans 10:9–10: That if thou shalt *confess with thy mouth the Lord Jesus,* and shalt believe in thine heart that God hath raised him from the dead, thou shalt be saved. For with the heart man believeth unto righteousness; and with the mouth confession is made unto salvation.

> Hebrews 12:27–28: And this word, yet once more, signifies the removing of those things that are shaken, as of things that are made, that those things which cannot

be shaken may remain. *Wherefore we, receiving a kingdom which cannot be moved, let us have grace, whereby we may serve God acceptably with reverence and godly fear.*

Given the nature of God's choice to pay the price for us and our choice to serve, we enter a lifelong familial commitment and covenant with each other. Within this relationship of family, we have chosen God to be a Patriarchal Father and Jesus to be our Lord and Master, who asks us to serve and obey. A master (*kurios*) is the possessor or owner of property or the head of a house. Being the "head" allows the master control of the persons—servants or slaves—within the household. To declare one our Lord or Master is to give complete authority or control, to make one supreme over all we have. This means that upfront, from the first moment of our salvation, we have declared our submission to Christ as Lord and Master, yet each day *we are still provided the choice* as to whether or not we will honor that profession and yield our lives in service to Him.

Because we retain our power of choice, our Master has detailed in scripture great rewards, current and future, that align with our decision to serve. Think of it this way: even though the Prodigal was welcomed back into and remained part of the family he left and returned to, he still missed out on years of benefits after wasting what he was given (Luke 15:11–32). We don't want to do the same; we don't want to waste any time away from the Father or throw away what has been promised by walking away from, instead of into, things of the kingdom. We serve a fair, loving, benevolent, and generous Father and a considerate and understanding Lord and Master, and all the conditions for benefits and rewards are well expressed in God's Word. Through the scriptures, we know what we have, we know how to receive it, and we are aware of how precious time is and how easy it is to waste it. *Our greatest risk is a life of missed spiritual opportunities to grow and to receive blessings of our inheritance in the here and now.* While we often focus on the long list of eternal rewards God has promised to bestow in eternity to those who serve him (Rev. 20), our inheritance is also released incrementally, in this world, very regularly and consistently, in response to our faith and the service to the kingdom we do while here on earth.

What we do, even for humanity, should reflect what we are doing for our Master. God is complete and self-sustaining; He doesn't need anything directly from us to make His life better. What He wants to see is us taking our place in His kingdom, being His ambassador, and using what He has given us for the benefit of His kingdom and His creation. God makes it clear that we have the right to choose what we will do with what He has given us, yet, if we choose to use it unwisely—to serve self and corruption—such uses will result in us being in bondage to keep serving a master that we were not meant to serve: money, power, or self (2 Pet. 2:19).

> John 12:25–26: He that loveth his life shall lose it; and he that hates his life in this world shall keep it unto life eternal. If any man serves me, let him follow me; and where I am, there shall also my servant be: if any man serves me, him will my Father honor.

> Colossians 3:23–25: And whatsoever ye do, do it heartily, as to the Lord, and not unto men; Knowing that of the Lord ye shall receive the reward of the inheritance: for ye serve the Lord Christ. But he that doeth wrong shall receive for the wrong which he hath done and there is no respect of persons.

> Matthew 25:31–46: When the Son of man shall come in his glory, and all the holy angels with him, then shall he sit upon the throne of his glory: And before him shall be gathered all nations: and he shall separate them one from another, as a shepherd divides his sheep from the goats: And he shall set the sheep on his right hand, but the goats on the left. Then shall the King say unto them on his right hand, Come, ye blessed of my Father, inherit the kingdom prepared for you from the foundation of the world: For I was hungry, and ye gave me meat: I was thirsty, and ye gave me drink: I was a stranger, and ye took me in: Naked, and ye clothed me: I was sick, and ye visited me: I was in prison, and ye came unto me. Then shall the righteous answer him, saying, Lord, when saw we thee hungry, and

fed thee? or thirsty, and gave thee drink? When saw we thee a stranger, and took thee in? or naked, and clothed thee? Or when saw we thee sick, or in prison, and came unto thee? And the King shall answer and say unto them, Verily I say unto you, inasmuch as ye have done it unto one of the least of these my brethren, ye have done it unto me. Then shall he say also unto them on the left hand, Depart from me, ye cursed, into everlasting fire, prepared for the devil and his angels: For I was an hungry, and ye gave me no meat: I was thirsty, and ye gave me no drink: I was a stranger, and ye took me not in: naked, and ye clothed me not: sick, and in prison, and ye visited me not. Then shall they also answer him, saying, Lord, when saw we thee hungry, or athirst, or a stranger, or naked, or sick, or in prison, and did not minister unto thee? Then shall he answer them, saying, Verily I say unto you, inasmuch as ye did it not to one of the least of these, ye did it not to me. And these shall go away into everlasting punishment: but the righteous into life eternal.

Malachi 3:17–18: And they shall be mine, saith the Lord of hosts, in that day when I make up my jewels; and I will spare them, as a man spares his own son that serves him. Then shall ye return, and discern between the righteous and the wicked, between him that serves God and him that serves him not.

The scripture above from Matthew 25 comes after a parable of not letting one's oil in the lamp burn out—a command to stay alert and ready while awaiting the Lord's return. There is also a parable to remind us to keep *multiplying* the talents He has given us by producing greater benefits for the kingdom with them. Each day is an opportunity to give and serve, and what we have here on earth is meant to generate even more benefits for the Master—which also produces gain for ourselves and others. We have a myriad of abilities that are meant to be used to bring the Master honor. In doing so, we aren't slaves but masters of our own lives, choosing what we will do and ultimately if we will use all of the resources we've been granted to serve another. That other should be the one who purchased us and provided us with the liberty to choose how our lives will benefit the kingdom.

In Matthew 4:10, we see the audacity of Satan trying to convince Jesus, God's Son, to use his gifts to serve self and Satan, to which Jesus provided the proper response, "Get thee hence, Satan: for it is written, thou shalt worship the Lord thy God, and Him only shalt thou serve." When we are confronted with the same choice, do we provide the same response? Do we contemplate whom or what we are serving with what we choose to do with our talents, love, and resources each day? Do we tell self and Satan to "get behind" when we know that he would be the only one to gain and that we would be denying the Father, the kingdom, and our position in heaven to take up the offer and option the enemy has placed before us?

> Galatians 5:13–14: For, brethren, ye have been called unto liberty; only use not liberty for an occasion to the flesh, but by love serve one another. For all the law is fulfilled in one word, even in this; Thou shalt love thy neighbor as thyself.

> 1 Peter 4:19: Wherefore, let them that suffer according to the will of God commit the keeping of their souls to him in well doing, as unto a faithful Creator.

> Matthew 6:24: No man can serve two masters: for either he will hate the one and love the other; or else he will hold to the one and despise the other. Ye cannot serve God and mammon (accumulation of wealth).

> Romans 1:25: Who changed the truth of God into a lie, and worshipped and served the creature more than the Creator, who is blessed forever. Amen.

God is our Father and our Creator; each of these truths leads us deeper into an awareness of our need to choose to live out who we were fearfully and wonderfully made to be (Ps. 139:14). With the knowledge and recognition of the price that was paid for us to live free from the condemnation of our sin also comes the choice to recognize Jesus not only as our Brother but also as our Lord and Master and to use our liberty, our freedom from slavery and bondage, to choose a life of service. Being released from our debt—for the wages of sin is death (Rom. 6:23)—also comes with inheriting a family value of paying forward and passing on forgiveness, love, and goodness. Being freed from that sentence and the bondage of selfishness gives us a mission of service that brings joy and purpose to our lives as our Master calls us to give what He has given and do what He has done. Jesus conveyed that in a parable he shared with his disciples that remains applicable today:

> Matthew 18:26–28: The servant therefore fell down, and worshipped him, saying, Lord, have patience with me, and I will pay thee all. Then the lord of that servant was moved with compassion, and loosed him, and forgave him the debt. But the same servant went out, and found one of his fellow servants, which owed him an hundred pence: and he laid hands on him, and took him by the throat, saying, Pay me what thou owes. And his fellow servant fell down at his feet, and besought him, saying, have patience with me, and I will pay thee all. And he would not: but went and cast him into prison, till he should pay the debt. So, when his fellow servants saw what was done, they were very sorry, and came and told unto their lord all that was done. Then his lord, after that he had called him, said unto him, O thou wicked servant, I forgave thee all that debt, because thou desired it of me: Shouldest not thou also have had compassion on thy fellow servant, even as I had pity on thee? And his lord was wroth, and delivered him to the tormentors, till he should pay all that was due unto him.

If we accepted the free gift of being purchased into grace, into being blood-bought and blood-washed, we entered into God's family by declaring Christ our Lord. Our Master is known to us. *He became our Master to save us from the destiny we had created for ourselves by serving ourselves.* With redemption, He gave us a new charge—to pick up our cross and follow

Him (Mark 8:34) and do the things He did. A disciple is never above his master nor a servant above his lord (Matt. 10:24), and yet Christ was a servant, showing the power of self-sacrifice for others. He openly professed the type of Master he would be, stating the "greatest among you shall be your servant" (Matt. 23:11). He washed the feet of those who called Him Master, and He demonstrated characteristics that make it easy for one's heart to choose to follow Him as a willing servant wanting to do the will of the Master while attempting to replicate His compassion and humility.

John 13:12–14: So after he had washed their feet, and had taken his garments, and was set down again, he said unto them, know ye what I have done to you? Ye call me Master and Lord: and ye say well; for so I am. If I then, your Lord and Master, have washed your feet; ye also ought to wash one another's feet.

Matthew 22:36–40: Master, which is the greatest commandment in the law? Jesus said unto him, thou shalt love the Lord thy God with all thy heart, and with all thy soul, and with all thy mind. This is the first and great commandment. And the second is like unto it, thou shalt love thy neighbor as thyself. On these two commandments hang all the law and the prophets.

Ephesians 6:5–9: Servants, be obedient to them that are your masters according to the flesh, with fear and trembling, in singleness of your heart, as unto Christ; Not with eyeservice, as men pleasers; but as the servants of Christ, doing the will of God from the heart; With good will doing service, as to the Lord, and not to men: knowing that whatsoever good thing any man doeth, the same shall he receive of the Lord, whether he be bond or free. And ye masters, do the same things unto them, forbearing threatening: knowing that your Master also is in heaven; neither is there respect of persons with him.

When we choose God, we choose a Master and a life of service. We then seek to live in a way that demonstrates the nature of our Master because of His influence in our lives and our yielding to His will. Our service becomes a lifelong pursuit of chasing His nature and doing good work—building our new identity in Christ for all to see. Service leads to development and the maturation process, and as that occurs, we become a better reflection of our Father and Brother. We become true disciples that follow in the pattern of our Master, who is a teacher, respected Lord, and friend.

> 2 Timothy 2:20–22: But in a great house there are not only vessels of gold and of silver, but also of wood and of earth; and some to honor, and some to dishonor. *If a man therefore purge himself from these, he shall be a vessel unto honor, sanctified, and meet for the master's use, and prepared unto every good work.* Flee also youthful lusts: but follow righteousness, faith, charity, peace, with them that call on the Lord out of a pure heart.

> Luke 9:23–24: And he said to them all, if any man will come after me, let him deny himself, and take up his cross daily, and follow me. For whosoever will save his life shall lose it: but whosoever will lose his life for my sake, the same shall save it.

This choice to serve and follow our Lord is ours to make, which ultimately distinguishes us as servants and not slaves; we have retained the choice to receive grace, and we are charged to wrestle with our free will to determine whom we will serve every day. *We are only bound to God by choice, by love, and by our acceptance of the amazing gift of salvation.* He willingly paid the price of admission for us to enter the kingdom while leaving the decision to walk through the door to us. Once we do, anything resembling slavery and bondage to another is meant to be left behind and be replaced with a life of service spurred by a grateful heart that desires to give back a small portion of all we have been given.

Reflection Questions

As you look back over the last year, has your life been a clear reflection of the Master you serve?

Have you considered yourself a disciple or follower of Christ as your Master? If so, how has your relationship with your Master been developed? How is He kept in the position of Lord over your life?

How can you be more intentional about using your time, talents, and treasure to honor the one who purchased you and redeemed you from a life of bondage to self and sin?

CHAPTER 8

NO MORE STRONGHOLDS!

Hopefully, the previous chapters have increased our confidence that we are sons and daughters, servants of the Most High God by choice, and not slaves to any other person or external influence that has been given or taken rights over us. We have a mighty position with God and the privilege and responsibility to access His kingdom to bring His power, strength, and love to this world. We share in the mighty ministry of reconciliation (2 Cor. 5:17–18), bringing things in this world into alignment with His desires. Yet, as we grow in embracing our identity and taking our position of strength and influence, we can sometimes have the greatest difficulty becoming master over one element that is ours to control—our flesh. Our Father knew that our greatest personal challenge would be managing our own mind, will, and emotions to resist temptations that have their origin *within* us. He provided us with a piece of His own nature, the Holy Spirit, to reside in us to influence our spirit and to lead us into a new way of thinking and being. We have been called and equipped to overcome our old carnal nature and to crucify it (Gal. 2:20), letting go of the old and becoming new. In Christ, we are no longer children of wrath (Eph. 2:2–3), being overcome by our desires and impulses and unknowingly surrendering to the prince of the powers of this earth. We are awake, we are aware, and we are empowered to overcome issues of the flesh. To do so, our will must be set to take the lead, steeled with a determination to follow the Spirit down a path to liberty and life and to empower us to use our God-shared authority to refuse to continue to be taken captive by anything *within us* that would hold us in bondage.

Galatians 5:13–26: For, brethren, *ye have been called unto liberty; only use not liberty for an occasion to the flesh, but by love serve one another.* For all the law is fulfilled in one word, even in this; Thou shalt love thy neighbor as thyself. But if ye bite and devour one another, take heed that ye be not consumed one of another. This I say then, *walk in the Spirit, and ye shall not fulfil the lust of the flesh.* For the flesh lusts against the Spirit, and the Spirit against the flesh: and these are contrary the one to the other: so that ye cannot do the things that ye would. But if ye be led of the Spirit, ye are not under the law. Now *the works of the flesh* are manifest, which are these; adultery, fornication, uncleanness, lasciviousness, idolatry, witchcraft, hatred, variance, emulations, wrath, strife, seditions, heresies, envying, murders, drunkenness, reveling, and such like: of the which I tell you before, as I have also told you in time past, that they which do such things shall not inherit the kingdom of God. But *the fruit of the Spirit* is love, joy, peace, longsuffering, gentleness, goodness, faith, meekness, temperance: against such there is no law. And *they that are Christ's have crucified the flesh with the affections and lusts.* If we live in the Spirit, let us also walk in the Spirit. Let us not be desirous of vain glory, provoking one another, envying one another.

Because of the Spirit in us, we have a companion, comforter, and partner in accessing the power and authority needed to overcome our carnal nature. We become the masters who bring the flesh into submission using all we have been given as joint heirs with our Lord and Master, embracing the fruits and gifts of the Spirit that exist in and for us to be transformed so we feel, think, and act as self-assured as Christ did when confronted with any temptation or challenge.

Being a slave in bondage creates three conditions:

1. A slave does not have a lasting position in the household one serves, nor does one's will matter to the master.

2. A slave hasn't chosen one's master, like servants choose whom they serve.
3. A mindset of slavery stays and invites ongoing bondage and submission to things one believes one cannot control.

As heirs, we bring thoughts and conditions into submission, overcoming any attempt to hold us in bondage to old ways of thinking and behaving.

Sin cannot defeat us. We, through the power of Christ, defeat it by the blood of the Lamb, the word of our testimony, and *by not loving our own opinion and ways* above God's (Rev. 12:11). We start this work by recognizing which thoughts we have held (many of these can be deep rooted and tied to strong emotions) that may be wrong and don't serve us well. What we believe about the temptations and risks around us tend to play out the way we expect them to because "as a person thinks in their heart" about themselves and the situation—they become (Prov. 23:7). Our sense of failure and frailty can have us start to succumb to thoughts that we cannot overcome or live victoriously; however, it is fixation on failures that may cause us to forget that we are part of God's family, His kingdom, and His church and that the gates of hell cannot prevail against us collectively or individually when we refuse to give up our position or identity in Christ (Matt. 16:18).

> 1 Corinthians 10:12–13: Wherefore let him that thinketh he stands, take heed lest he fall. There hath no temptation taken you, but such as is common to man: but God is faithful, who will not suffer you to be tempted above that ye are able; but will with the temptation also make a way to escape, that ye may be able to bear it.

> Matthew 18:18–19: Verily I say unto you, whatsoever ye shall bind on earth shall be bound in heaven: and whatsoever ye shall loose on earth shall be loosed in heaven. Again, I say unto you, that if two of you shall agree on earth as touching anything that they shall ask, it shall be done for them of my Father which is in heaven.

Very often, we expect our Father God to protect us from the evil, to keep it from us so we are not tempted, yet the opposite is promised. James 1 speaks clearly that we are to expect temptations and challenges in this life and that we are expected to develop and mature and not be derailed by those challenges. In these cases, the focus is not meant to be on the conditions and external influences coming at or upon us but on our ability to manage our mind, will, and emotions in response to what is occurring around or to us.

> James 1:2–16: My brethren, count it all joy when ye fall into diverse temptations; Knowing this, that the *trying of your faith* worketh patience. But let patience have her perfect work, that ye may be perfect and entire, wanting nothing. If any of you lack wisdom, let him ask of God, that giveth to all men liberally, and upbraids not; and it shall be given him. But let him ask in faith, nothing wavering. For he that wavers is like a wave of the sea driven with the wind and tossed. For let not that man think that he shall receive anything of the Lord. A double minded man is unstable in all his ways. Let the brother of low degree rejoice in that he is exalted: But the rich, in that he is made low: because as the flower of the grass he shall pass away. For the sun is no sooner risen with a burning heat, but it withers the grass, and the flower thereof fall, and the grace of the fashion of it perishes: so also shall the rich man fade away in his ways. *Blessed is the man that endures temptation: for when he is tried, he shall receive the crown of life,* which the Lord hath promised to them that love him. Let no man say when he is tempted, I am tempted of God: for God cannot be tempted with evil, neither tempts he any man: *But every man is tempted, when he is drawn away of his own lust, and enticed.* Then when lust hath conceived, it bringeth forth sin: and sin, when it is finished, bringeth forth death. Do not err, my beloved brethren.

Note in the above scripture that God, through James, is urging us to have faith in ourselves and in our partnership with the Holy Spirit to resist temptations and old things of our carnal nature. We are called to draw on the fruit of the Holy Spirit within us to reject the thoughts, desires, and lusts meant to destroy us. Guilt and shame can arise when we yield to something that may be immediately gratifying but ultimately cause harm by eroding our faith in ourselves and our identity as victors. The battles we enter are meant to be won to continuously build self-control and confidence. We start this process of victory within by first *believing that we can* dismiss and capture stray thoughts and old desires one by one. Once we know our capacity for self-determination and self-control, we start to live out being who we envision and desire ourselves to be in Christ.

Think of young adults who are living on their own for the first time. They will be out of their parents' home and exposed to many new opportunities. They can fully make their own choices and are now able to determine what they value, who they are, and what consequences they are willing to risk. It is the process of recognizing *why* one is pulled toward an influence and contemplating *the reasons not to yield* that foster ownership of decision-making and spiritual maturation. Similarly, our Father is looking for us to grow up, to apply what He has taught us, for us to take authority over our old nature, and to proclaim who we are in Him. As a child in God's kingdom, we have been trained in the way we should go; we have spiritual knowledge of what is right and have been endued with the power and strength to do so. We have been given the authority to proclaim, declare, bind, loose, and conquer to prevail against internal and external influences, and so we are often led into a decision point—will we do what we know we *should* do, or will we *surrender ourselves* to what erodes our transformation into an heir who wields the power and influence of the kingdom?

It starts with self-assessment: Do we believe we can do what is right? Do we expect to follow the leading of the Spirit? Generally, *what we expect, we will do*—and we know that faith without works is dead (James 2:18–26). *We are equipped to set our beliefs on our ability to prevail and then act quickly in alignment with that belief.* We must capture and reorder our thoughts, establishing our expectation to overcome and then move in the direction that our faith takes us. Our spiritual identity is one of power and strength, one of confidence that we can and will boldly take dominion over everything God has given us to control in our own lives—which is quite a bit. We have been given a will to manage our mind and emotions; we have been given a Spirit to lead us. We have joined a family that provides fellowship, support, and guidance, and we are meant to connect with and pray for one another (James 5:16), which is God's way of ensuring we aren't alone in this battle. We are always at the crossroad of deciding whom and what we will yield ourselves to. We will either submit to or resist impulse and desire using the will and authority God has given us. The more regularly we contain and train the flesh, the less powerful its influence is over time. The more disciplined and intentional we are to control the flesh, the more it incrementally dies as it was meant to when we stepped into being our Father's child (Col. 1:22).

This is our greatest responsibility and challenge as we are always renewing, transforming, and maturing into kingdom thinking and living. *We are building up our spiritual identity to compete with our carnal one.* The enemy would want us to believe that this is a battle we cannot win and that we'll always be tempted beyond what we can resist, yet God has instructed us to put on an armor of protection to *cover our own mind and heart* against thoughts and attacks that would hurt us. He is confident that we can stand on the front lines and be able to walk in peace through all situations. Do we see ourselves that way? Do we hold the shield of faith (confidence and assurance) high and refuse to let it drop when we think of our ability to resist negativity? Or when weak, beggarly, and slavish thinking hits? Are we warriors who know that every arrow launched against our hearts, minds, and the truth *will be* quenched before it can do any damage? We are charged to *fight* the good fight of faith (1 Tim. 6:12), knowing that God has made us able—more than able—to resist, stand, fight, and prevail. *The more we have faith in that knowledge, the more our actions will prove it out each day by holding firm to our confidence in God and ourselves in everything we face.* Numbers 13–14 teaches us that the report we provide based on what we see will either be good or bad. Caleb confessed, "Let us go up at once, and possess it; for we are well able to overcome it," while others looked at the promised land and determined that they stood as grasshoppers in a land of giants. The report we provide ourselves should be formed by our understanding of God's promises and our position in

Christ and not be formed by a detrimental assessment of what we consider the giants in our lives to be. *Our fight is our battle to keep our faith in our God-given abilities high and strong, to overcome our own self-doubt and fear of failure and vulnerability.* When we keep the shield in position, we keep our faith intact, and we can then stand still, letting the promises of God move from heaven to earth on our behalf. When we master this work, it is then that we regularly begin to see many things *in us* and our lives that were hoped for but previously unseen.

> Romans 6:13–15: Neither yield ye your members as instruments of unrighteousness unto sin: but yield yourselves unto God, as those that are alive from the dead, and your members as instruments of righteousness unto God. *For sin shall not have dominion over you*: for ye are not under the law, but under grace. What then? shall we sin, because we are not under the law, but under grace? God forbid.

> James 4:7: Submit yourselves therefore to God. Resist the devil, and he will flee from you.

> Romans 12:21: Be not overcome of evil but overcome evil with good.

> Ephesians 6:10–18: Finally, my brethren, be strong in the Lord, and in the power of his might. Put on the whole armor of God, that ye may be able to stand against the wiles of the devil. For we wrestle not against flesh and blood, but against principalities, against powers, against the rulers of the darkness of this world, against spiritual wickedness in high places. Wherefore take unto you the whole armor of God, that ye may be able to withstand in the evil day, and having done all, to stand. Stand therefore, having your loins girt about with truth, and having on the breastplate of righteousness; and your feet shod with the preparation of the gospel of peace; above all, taking

the shield of faith, wherewith ye shall be able to quench all the fiery darts of the wicked. And take the helmet of salvation, and the sword of the Spirit, which is the word of God: Praying always with all prayer and supplication in the Spirit and watching thereunto with all perseverance and supplication for all saints.

When we believe in our own power and capacities (because God has given them to us and made us to be more than conquerors), we can recognize and overcome each errant thought that is meant to entrap us or shift our focus away from understanding and operating in our spiritual identity. Every challenge gives us an opportunity to either respond from our frail and impulsive carnal nature, which can easily be overwhelmed and negatively influenced, or to fix our minds and focus on our spiritual identity and our spiritual tools. Everything promised to us in terms of victory over emotions (such as fear and doubt) is activated by us doing our part to embrace the promise through faith and to apply it through action. When we use the tools given us, like putting on the armor of God, we are able to remain assured and confident that we can *handle what is happening within us well enough to address what is happening around us more effectively and successfully.* Putting on the armor of God noted in Ephesians 6 is ultimately a change of one's mindset; it is a recognition that despite what is occurring, our righteous position in God has not changed. We walk into a situation peaceful and calm because we know what the gospel says, and we know beyond a shadow of a doubt that every fiery dart will be quenched and that we are able to stand before God without shame or blame. Reading God's Word to know and understand these truths is ultimately what allows us to apply this knowledge quickly in any situation meant to test how strong our armor is and how deep our confidence goes. We often focus on the weapons used *against* us; however, we have our own weapons in this fight of faith, and a weapon is only as functional as the person who wields it. Do we have strength to hold the shield of faith for a minute, an hour, or a day? Do we have the sword of God's Word ready to be spoken quickly and directly into or at a problem? Do we adeptly grab hold of a rising lie or ill-intended thought, take it captive, and reduce it into nothingness by comparing it to the truth of God's Word? As in all aspects of life, practice improves our skills and abilities, and that includes our ability to resist temptation, overcome evil, and discern the voice of the Spirit that consistently and adeptly leads us toward life and peace.

> 2 Corinthians 10:4–6: (For the weapons of our warfare are not carnal, but mighty through God to the pulling down of strongholds;) *Casting down imaginations*, and every high thing that exalts itself against the knowledge of God, and *bringing into captivity* every thought to the obedience of Christ; And having in *a readiness to revenge all disobedience*, when your obedience is fulfilled.

> Romans 8:6–8: For to be carnally minded is death; but *to be spiritually minded is life and peace*. Because the carnal mind is enmity against God: for it is not subject to the law of God, neither indeed can be. So, then they that are in the flesh cannot please God.

We often read terms in scripture that relate to our "flesh" and "carnal" mind and nature. Carnal (GK: *sarx*) is to live within the restrictions and desires of one's body; it is to only know the frailties, interests, needs, and limitations of one's human nature, as if it were the only real thing or the only need to be satisfied. *It is responding to life as if our thoughts, our needs, and our desires are all right and the only thing that matters*, which is why serving the carnal nature is basically a path to selfishness, pride, and self-destruction (Prov. 16:18). Because we think or feel something doesn't automatically make it true or worthy of pursuit. Many of our reactionary responses are meant to pull us back into old ways instead of releasing us to live in newness. We must grow in the knowledge of the Word of God to be good discerners of which voice, thought, and desire we should follow:

> 1 Corinthians 2:14: But the natural man receives not the things of the Spirit of God: for they are foolishness unto him: neither can he know them, because they are spiritually discerned.

Hebrews 4:12: For the word of God is quick, and powerful, and sharper than any two-edged sword, piercing even to the dividing asunder of soul and spirit, and of the joints and marrow, and is a discerner of the thoughts and intents of the heart.

Hebrews 5:14: But strong meat belongs to them that are of full age, even those who by reason of use have their senses exercised to discern both good and evil.

Awaking our spirit, through salvation and regeneration (John 3), changes us to become as originally intended, a spirit that has a soul that lives in a body who can fellowship with God, our Father, and be part of a family that knows how to love, care, and sacrifice for one another. We must embrace being a new creature redesigned to grow and prevail over old carnal ways. Whatever thoughts try to hold us in bondage to our old nature must be challenged. Any *feelings* that we cannot resist or change, must themselves be resisted. We are the gatekeepers of what "old" carnal beliefs we allow to remain and what "new" spiritually discerned thoughts we choose to embrace. Any thought that diminishes our knowledge of who we are in Christ must be isolated, taken captive, and cast down. In doing so, we ultimately come to learn and grow in our spiritual authority and strength. We become aligned with the new amazing design God has always seen us to be from the moment of creation. We grow stronger and truer to this identity each time we *take revenge* on any influence that led us into disobedience in the past, and we build a stronger conviction that we can be even more obedient to the things of God in the future. It was this revelation that allowed Paul to write his letter to the Philippians, charging them to stand fast, rejoice, be careful about nothing, stand in peace, think good thoughts, and be content, because those who have joined the kingdom "can do all things through Christ which strengthens us." If you need a boost in confidence, read all of Philippians chapter 4; God inspired Paul to relay a list of charges to us. If we follow them, we will be able to manage our internal fight with the flesh to achieve self-control and victory and grow stronger, bolder, and more transformed and representative of the kingdom of God every day.

We must learn to stop accepting thoughts that tear us down and hold us down, including those thoughts that tell us that we are failures because we still battle our flesh. We will make mistakes as we are works in progress (Phil. 1:6); the key is to learn from them and let them make us better. We cannot do all we are charged to do in our own strength, but we can and will do what we need to do through Christ, who strengthens us *in the inner man*, and with the Spirit that dwells within us that shares His nature of self-control with us. *The old nature will want to remain or return, but it is meant to pass away. We are active participants in bringing forth that crucifixion so that we can build up, resurrect, and embrace what is new, spiritual, and powerful about us.* Living in newness of life is the inheritance of being a new creation in Christ.

> Ephesians 3:19–21: And to know the love of Christ, which passes knowledge, that ye might be filled with all the fulness of God. Now unto him that is able to do exceedingly abundantly above all that we ask or think, *according to the power that worketh in us,* unto him be glory in the church by Christ Jesus throughout all ages, world without end. Amen.

> Colossians 1:10–12: That ye might walk worthy of the Lord unto all pleasing, being fruitful in every good work, and increasing in the knowledge of God; *strengthened with all might, according to his glorious power, unto all patience and longsuffering with joyfulness*; giving thanks unto the Father, which hath made us meet to be partakers of the inheritance of the saints in light.

> 2 Corinthians 13:3–5: Since ye seek a proof of Christ speaking in me, which to you-ward is not weak, but is mighty in you. For though he was crucified through weakness, yet he lives by the power of God. For we also are weak in him, *but we shall live with him by the power of God* toward you. Examine yourselves, whether ye be in the

faith; prove your own selves. Know ye not your own selves, how that Jesus Christ is in you, except ye be reprobates?

Life is our opportunity to prove to ourselves that we are more than able. We must let the Holy Spirit lead and guide us into learning how to be victorious over the "old" us so we can embrace the strong, courageous, bold, and influential us that Christ died for us to be and which our Father envisioned for us to be when we were fearfully and wonderfully made. We were created in the image of God (Gen. 1:27), and now, through Christ, we are empowered to overcome any and all old thoughts and ways that would keep us from loving and serving Him with all our heart, soul, mind, and strength. *There is nothing binding us or holding us back that our spiritual nature in Christ cannot overcome.* See it, believe it, live it!

> 1 John 5:3–5: For this is the love of God, that we keep his commandments: and his commandments are not grievous. For *whatsoever is born of God overcomes the world*: and this is the victory that overcomes the world, even our faith. Who is he that overcomes the world, but he that believeth that Jesus is the Son of God?

We are no longer slaves to sin. We are overcomers of the world and our flesh, and our victory starts with faith, not just in God but also in whom He has designed, equipped, and empowered us to be. We must keep identifying, casting out, taking revenge on, and overcoming errant thoughts and old ways until there are no more strongholds standing in the way of us embracing our full identity in Christ.

Reflection Questions

Are there certain negative thoughts about yourself that keep rising up, taking a higher position of influence in your mind than they should?

How do you identify them?

How do you take them captive, cast them down, and replace them with spiritual truth?

What areas do you feel like you are an overcomer, and in what areas do you feel like you need to build your faith to experience confidence and assurance that you can and will prevail?

What action will you take to build your faith in those areas?

CHAPTER 9

GREAT IN GOD

By challenging our mindset and no longer thinking like beggars and slaves, we can walk in the greatness God has called us to. If we are freed from limitations and insecurities, we can read and embrace scriptures that invite us to live boldly:

- As children who have a marvelous position in the family of God.
- In fellowship with Christ as joint heirs with Him while honoring His position as Lord.
- In fellowship with others, giving and receiving benefits from one another's design.
- In obedience to God, seeking to serve, learn, and grow progressively as a way of life.
- In partnership with the Holy Spirit, embracing the love and goodness of God in us that empowers us to be successful overcomers of all that might challenge us.
- In fellowship with God the Father, Christ our Lord and Master, and the Holy Spirit, which opens the way for us to experience newness of life, filled with abundance and opportunities that exceed what is possible and available to us on our own.

Our spiritual identity will be small or great based on what we know about our privilege and power in Christ. Do we see ourselves as grasshoppers or giants in a land flowing with milk and honey? Do we see ourselves as victors, conquerors, and overcomers of internal, physical, and spiritual battles? This book has hopefully given you the opportunity to pause and evaluate unhealthy and unhelpful beliefs that linger beyond salvation that may be compromising your ability to live out your spiritual identity and receive your full spiritual inheritance. Think how great life is and could be if we were all able to free ourselves of weak and beggarly thoughts— thoughts that hold us in bondage, hold us down, and leave us desperate and desolate. Instead, what if we all walked in faith, fought the good fight of faith, and shed negative thoughts and deflected fiery darts as quickly as they arrived?

Proverbs 23:7 says that "as a man thinketh in his heart, so is he." This truth comes with a charge that is the key to our success. To think (Hebrew: *shaar*) means to literally split open and decide to allow in. We are gatekeepers as to what we allow into our hearts. We are meant to calculate the cost and risk of what we allow access to our most innermost place, our heart. We are meant to be *miserly and protective* of our heart. We are to judiciously manage what goes in, knowing it will influence what beliefs, words, and actions come out. Do we slam the gate shut on fears and insecurity and doubt? Do we open our hearts wide to the truth of the Word? *Our ability and responsibility to gatekeep what we focus on puts the control of our lives, peace, and identity in our hands.* We are equipped, charged, and empowered to question and manage our perspective of life, which determines how we see and interact with the world. Our thoughts govern how we speak to ourselves and others and the actions we choose to take out of those convictions. God has given us free will to choose how to handle our thoughts and endowed us with strength and provided His Word so we could be victorious on the battlefield of the mind. Choice is a tricky master; it is ours to tame and wield, by exercising discernment and following the leading of the Holy Spirit. We are meant to meditate upon the Word of God, our calling and spiritual identity, and the provision of God, like as was charged to Timothy (1 Tim. 4:14–15). The more we do so, the more we will think and believe what God says about us and pursue what He wants us to know. We will be properly focused and fixed on the gift of being His child, His servant, and His heir unto the promises. In short, we must assertively, continuously, and faithfully let the Word of God into our hearts until we fully believe it and our lives reflect it.

> Luke 6:45: A good man out of the good treasure of his heart
> bringeth forth that which is good; and an evil man out of
> the evil treasure of his heart bringeth forth that which is
> evil: for of the abundance of the heart his mouth speaks.

We are called to live intentionally. We must continue to strip out the old and replace it with the new until our heart holds so much treasure of goodness and faith that the abundance in it flows naturally from our tongues. We will be able to "be still and know that He is God" (Ps. 46:10) even in the most trying times, just as King David was able to amid some extremely difficult moments. We will humble ourselves before God when we've done wrong or life is beyond our control, knowing that He will lift us up in due time (James 4:10). We will stand firm and confident in a good outcome simply because God says so and we expect our Father to act true to His Word.

Our thoughts can take all types of forms, and we must gatekeep to ensure we are only giving the proper ones access to our innermost being. We must constantly evaluate the thoughts in our head prior to allowing them residency in our heart. If we meditate, like Joshua, on the scriptures that confirm that we are more than able, we can then take bold risks and find the blessings that come from living in the promises and inheritance of God (Josh. 1:8). Perhaps some of the greatest secrets to unlocking great thinking are found throughout the book of Matthew.

> Matthew 6:32–34: (For after all these things do the
> Gentiles seek:) for your heavenly Father knows that ye
> have need of all these things. *But seek ye first the kingdom
> of God*, and his righteousness; and all these things shall be
> added unto you. *Take therefore no thought for the morrow*:
> for the morrow shall take thought for the things of itself.
> Sufficient unto the day is the evil thereof.

Within this scripture, we are told to seek (search out by any method, pursue until we find) the kingdom of God *first*. Seek to understand what God's Word says, what His purpose for us is, what His promises are, what our position is *first* before allowing any other thoughts a prominent place in our decision-making and in our emotional response. If we seek kingdom wisdom *first*, we won't be burdened, drowned, or overwhelmed by other concerns. In fact, the truth of God is the only thing we are meant to meditate on and give access to our hearts; we should throw open the gates widely to the truth while being miserly against thoughts that create cares, fears, worries, and doubts. "Take no thought (GK: *merimnao*) for the morrow" is literally stating not to receive any mental mindset that creates anxiety or reduces our hope and confidence in what lies ahead. We know that cares are meant to be *immediately* cast off (1 Pet. 5:7) and made subject to God by recognizing that He cares for us and already knows everything we have need of. When we seek God first (GK: *proton*), we are putting Him, His Word, and His ways ahead of all and before all. This word *first* is all inclusive of time, order, placement, and importance. When the Word is first, the cares, concerns, and facts of the world's restrictions become secondary and remain in that demoted position. His thoughts are and remain higher than our thoughts (Isa. 55:9), and when they are ranked and held in the proper position, we can then gatekeep the pathway into our hearts much more effectively. If we ask for the wisdom and control of the Holy Spirit and seek God's will and way first, we are sure to find Him and to receive a response of good things from heaven, which our Father is eager to provide.

> Matthew 7:7–12: Ask, and it shall be given you; seek, and ye shall find; knock, and it shall be opened unto you: For every one that asks receives; and he that seeks finds; and to him that knocks it shall be opened. Or what man is there of you, whom if his son asks for bread, will he give him a stone? Or if he asks for a fish, will he give him a serpent? If ye then, being evil, know how to give good gifts unto your children, how much more shall your Father which is in heaven give good things to them that ask him? Therefore, all things whatsoever ye would that men should do to you, do ye even so to them: for this is the law and the prophets.

We find God when we think upon Him, when we open the Word of God and ponder its meaning. It happens when we sit in quiet prayer and reflection and when we feverously cry at his feet. It happens when we turn to Him, not just with our own opinions, needs, and pains fueling our outpouring but also by *seeking* the truth that will set us free. There must be an exchange of us for Him, old for new, natural for supernatural, and the relinquishing of our opinions and nature for the redeeming grace and strength of God. We don't go to God to reinforce our opinion of the problem; we come seeking to find a spiritual solution based on our spiritual identity and the abundance of the kingdom.

We can only find God's truth by diving in and *abiding in* His Word and choosing to follow the instruction within it as disciples, as ones committed to doing our part in receiving the promises (John 8:31–32). *We must intentionally find and stay focused on our spiritual position to let that knowledge convict and convince us.* As it does, it will penetrate and permeate our hearts. If the right thoughts live in our hearts, our existence will be more and more reflective of the person our Father God made and called us to be. We will realize that the crown on our head makes us just a little lower than the angels, in a position of glory and honor, with *this world subject to us*, because we are joint heirs with Christ (Heb. 2:6–8). He gave us the power to think. It is an amazing ability with amazing consequences and "to whom much is given, much is required." We have been given much. We have been made children, but we have also been offered heirship if we mature into understanding and using those rights. We have been charged to seek out this inheritance—to know and access it to the fullest. We know that the journey is walked as an act of faith and that without faith it is impossible to please Him (God); for he that comes to God must believe that He is, and that He is a rewarder of them that *diligently seek* Him (Heb. 11:6). Many of us have come to God, but do we diligently seek Him? Do we know Him as Father and conveyor of the inheritance? Do we persist in learning about and pursuing all He has for us?

The journey of understanding and embracing one's spiritual identity is a lifelong one that is filled with daily steps on our faith walk. Each day, we meter, monitor, and gatekeep our thoughts, constantly renewing our minds—shifting old, ugly, harmful, limiting, carnal thoughts out and replacing them with the knowledge of truth, love, hope, power, strength, goodness, and righteousness. It is by changing our thoughts and mitigating their influence on the heart that we get to prove—live out—the good, acceptable, and perfect will of God in our lives.

Romans 12:1–3: I beseech you therefore, brethren, by the mercies of God, that ye present your bodies a living sacrifice, holy, acceptable unto God, which is your reasonable service. And be not conformed to this world: but be ye transformed *by the renewing of your mind, that ye may prove what is that good, and acceptable, and perfect, will of God.* For I say, through the grace given unto me, to every man that is among you, not to think of himself more highly than he ought to think; *but to think soberly,* according as God hath dealt to every man the measure of faith.

Notice that Paul challenges us to "think soberly." This type of thinking (GK: *phroneo*) is to exercise the mind in an intentional way. It is saying to set our minds in a predisposed direction—to interest ourselves in and to put on a certain mind set. In this case, it is the mindset of faith and our spiritual identity that we are meant to put on each day. He follows to say that God has given us a measure of faith—of confidence, assurance, and conviction—that we are meant to build on. *That lets us know that what we are to be intentional about is our level of faith and how much we embrace the knowledge of all we are capable of knowing and doing beyond our own abilities because of who we are in Christ.* If we don't transform our thinking, we will continue conforming to this world, and our carnal nature will remain intact or even grow. We won't realize our spiritual identity or inheritance until our mind finds and embraces what God has for us. This scripture reveals *why* we have been given a powerful will and the right to make our own choices—it is for us to embrace our responsibility to renew our minds and gatekeep our thoughts effectively so we can have the life and impact God desires us to have. By thinking soberly, we insert our will to intentionally, quickly, and effectively align our opinion and mindset with God's truth, with a new attitude emboldened by our position and the partnership we have with Christ our Lord and the Holy Spirit that dwells within. We can use our gatekeeping abilities to take on the same mind as Christ (Phil. 2), to become both humble and strong, loving and fierce, yielded and determined. When we renew our minds, we replace the reactive, opinionated carnal way we normally think with a thoughtful, focused new approach to living as a child of a loving Father and as brethren of the mightiest King.

If we have let negative, harmful thoughts linger in our hearts too long, it will take time and work to identify and remove them. If we have allowed thoughts that refuse to let light, love, and truth into our hearts or thoughts that keep us from seeking, finding, and living out the good, acceptable, and perfect will of God in our lives, we must recognize them as barriers to embracing our spiritual identity. Those thoughts are strongholds that need to be taken captive, brought down, and made obedient to God's Word (2 Cor. 10:5) - And God has given you the power and capacity to do so.

Now, we return to the question we began with, hoping that we all know God and feel more known of Him as well after taking this journey together. We pause to ponder if we will continue to allow ourselves *to turn back again* to those things we were made free of through God's gift of salvation. Do we still have or invite the weak and beggarly elements and those that enslave us to remain in our minds and hearts?

> Galatians 4:9: But now, after that ye have known God, or rather are known of God, how turn ye again to the weak and beggarly elements, whereunto ye desire again to be in bondage?

The key to bolstering and embracing our spiritual identity in Christ is to set our hearts and minds on what is spiritual, what is above, and what is lasting, and to hold fast to it in faith and fight any influence, urge, and thought that would distract, detract, or betray our conviction to be all God has made and called us to be. Do we think like Christ, our Master and joint heir, thinks? Do we hold fast to the Word of God and keep the promises of God in *first* position no matter how many competing facts, alternative opinions, and temptations arise?

> 1 Corinthians 2:15–16: But he that is spiritual judges all things, yet he himself is judged of no man. For who hath known the mind of the Lord, that he may instruct him? but we have the mind of Christ.

1 Peter 5:9–10: Whom resist steadfast in the faith, knowing that the same afflictions are accomplished in your brethren that are in the world. But the God of all grace, who hath called us unto his eternal glory by Christ Jesus, after that ye have suffered a while, make you perfect, stablish, strengthen, settle you.

1 Thessalonians 5:21: Prove all things; hold fast that which is good.

2 Timothy 1:12–14: For which cause I also suffer these things: nevertheless I am not ashamed: for I know whom I have believed, and am persuaded that he is able to keep that which I have committed unto him against that day. *Hold fast the form of sound words, which thou hast heard of me, in faith and love which is in Christ Jesus.* That good thing which was committed unto thee keep by the Holy Ghost which dwelleth in us.

When we fix ourselves on being steadfast in our knowledge and faith, God will always bring us back to a place of perfection (where we are supposed to be in Him), to the place He established for us to be in His kingdom, to a place of strength, where our soul is settled in peace and confidence. The more we check our thoughts to ensure we aren't conforming to negativity, bondage, weakness, and beggarly views, the quicker we can reject and replace those thoughts with new ones built on faith and spiritual strength. Cares will be cast away, damaging thoughts will be taken captive, and our hearts will be protected as we gatekeep out the thoughts of what we cannot do and replace them with the knowledge that "with God, nothing is impossible" (Matt. 17:20). We will be able to "be careful for nothing" and to experience rising and consistent confidence and assurances in our inheritance as promised by God, for both today and into eternity.

Philippians 4:6–8: Be careful for nothing; but in everything by prayer and supplication with thanksgiving let your requests be made known unto God. And the

95

peace of God, which passes all understanding, *shall keep your hearts and minds* through Christ Jesus. Finally, brethren, whatsoever things are true, whatsoever things are honest, whatsoever things are just, whatsoever things are pure, whatsoever things are lovely, whatsoever things are of good report; if there be any virtue, and if there be any praise, *think on these things.*

2 Timothy 1:7: For God hath not given us the spirit of fear; but of power, and of love, and of a sound mind.

As we read God's Word, we must consider the mindset He has called us to have. We must intentionally and soberly assess our thoughts each day, especially when under stress or in crisis. Soberly (GK: *sophronos*) translates to a sound mind, which takes *all things* in moderation—sipping so we can spit out what we shouldn't take in and allowing ourselves to only drink deep of the living water that can refresh and sustain our soul. God has given us the charge to renew our minds so we can have clear and uncluttered thoughts. He instructs us on what to receive, what to reject, and what to resist. The more we read His Word, the more clarity we receive, which allows us to remove what does not belong and does not serve us well.

John had a special relationship with Christ. He saw things differently from the other disciples, and because he did, he lived differently. He had a strong understanding of his spiritual position and identity in Christ, and he viewed the world through lenses of love, light, and power. He managed his thoughts and perspective; he renewed his mind and soberly directed his thoughts toward understanding his place in God's family and kingdom. He meditated on what it meant to be "born of God" and to live a life of service and victory through faith. He gives us a great example of a sober, spiritual mindset:

1 John 5:1–12: Whosoever believeth that Jesus is the Christ is born of God: and everyone that loveth him that begat loveth him also that is begotten of him. By this we know that we love the children of God, when we love God, and keep his commandments. For this is

the love of God, that we keep his commandments: and his commandments are not grievous. For *whatsoever is born of God overcomes the world: and this is the victory that overcomes the world, even our faith.* Who is he that overcomes the world, but he that believeth that Jesus is the Son of God? This is he that came by water and blood, even Jesus Christ; not by water only, but by water and blood. And it is *the Spirit that bears witness, because the Spirit is truth.* For there are three that bear record in heaven, the Father, the Word, and the Holy Ghost: and these three are one. And there are three that bear witness in earth, the Spirit, and the water, and the blood: and these three agree in one. If we receive the witness of men, the witness of God is greater: for this is the witness of God which he hath testified of his Son. He that believeth on the Son of God hath the witness in himself: he that believeth not God hath made him a liar; because he believeth not the record that God gave of his Son. And this is the record, that God hath given to us eternal life, and this life is in his Son. *He that hath the Son hath life*; and he that hath not the Son of God hath not life.

We are a witness to the world by demonstrating the power of God in us. To be a witness (GK: *martus*) is to testify to the truths we know and what we have heard and seen. We are to speak of what God has done in and through us. A witness provides a report that gives proof to a claim that has been made. In this case, we are meant to be witnesses and to testify to others about what God, our Father, has done by giving Him the ability to do exceedingly abundantly above all we can ask or think in our lives through His power at work *in us*. We bring the light that combats the darkness, the salt that flavors the earth, and we prove God's good and perfect will for His children by living in it each day. Our spiritual identity brings us into an amazing family and kingdom, which provides a witness for the world to see; it draws others toward us who want to know the reason we think, speak, and act differently.

John 17:10–15: And all mine are thine, and thine are mine; and I am glorified in them. And now I am no more in the world, but these are in the world, and I come to thee. Holy Father, keep through thine own name those whom thou hast given me, that they may be one, as we are … And now come I to thee; and these things I speak in the world, that *they might have my joy fulfilled in themselves*. I have given them thy word; and the world hath hated them, because they are not of the world, even as I am not of the world. I pray not that thou shouldest take them out of the world, but that thou shouldest keep them from evil.

God desires for us to think spiritually and embrace our spiritual identity in Him. This is something Paul sought to convey and convince the Corinthians, writing it down so all who seek God could find and learn from it as well. From the day of salvation, we are moved to transform and to embrace our new spiritual identity, moving from carnal things, from "milk" to "meat" of spiritual knowledge, so we can grow strong in the Lord and the power of His might (Eph. 6:10).

1 Corinthians 3:1–8: And I, brethren, could not speak unto you as unto spiritual, but as unto carnal, even as unto babes in Christ. I have fed you with milk, and not with meat: for hitherto ye were not able to bear it, neither yet now are ye able. For ye are yet carnal: for whereas there is among you envying, and strife, and divisions, are ye not carnal, and walk as men? For while one saith, I am of Paul; and another, I am of Apollos; are ye not carnal? Who then is Paul, and who is Apollos, but ministers by whom ye believed, even as the Lord gave to every man? I have planted, Apollos watered; but God gave the increase. So then neither is he that plants anything, neither he that waters; but God that giveth the increase. Now he that plants and he that waters are one: and *every man shall receive his own reward according to his own labor*.

Note in these first verses that our spiritual identity is supposed to be distinguishable from those without Christ, who are not part of God's family. We are to labor as children in the family and servants of our Lord, helping to produce an increase of kingdom influence in this world. And while God is the one that gives the increase, He is committed to rewarding us for stepping into the role He has given us in the family of God and His kingdom, empowering us to make a visible difference here on earth.

> 1 Corinthians 3:9–13: For we are laborers together with God: ye are God's husbandry, ye are God's building. According to the grace of God which is given unto me, as a wise master builder, I have laid the foundation, and another builds thereon. But let every man take heed how he builds thereupon. For other foundation can no man lay than that is laid, which is Jesus Christ. Now if any man build upon this foundation gold, silver, precious stones, wood, hay, stubble; Every man's work shall be made manifest: for the day shall declare it, because it shall be revealed by fire; and the fire shall try every man's work of what sort it is.

While salvation is a free gift and Christ is our firm foundation, *what gets built on top of the foundation is ours to determine.* Our will and faith will determine how high we build and with what materials—straw, wood, or precious stones. We cannot serve both God and mammon. We know that only what is done for God registers in heaven before our Father and is evaluated for His final determination of "well-done though good and faithful servant." We shouldn't fear the moment we stand before Him with our works being tried by fire, knowing that we pursued our spiritual identity and our spiritual calling to its fullest, taking advantage of all our Father gave us to have, to be, and to do.

> 1 Corinthians 3:14–23: If any man's work abide which he hath built thereupon, he shall receive a reward. If any man's work shall be burned, he shall suffer loss: but he himself shall be saved; yet so as by fire. Know ye not

that ye are the temple of God, and that the Spirit of God dwelleth in you? If any man defile the temple of God, him shall God destroy; for the temple of God is holy, which temple ye are. Let no man deceive himself. If any man among you seems to be wise in this world, let him become a fool, that he may be wise. For the wisdom of this world is foolishness with God. For it is written, He taketh the wise in their own craftiness. And again, The Lord knows the thoughts of the wise, that they are vain. Therefore, let no man glory in men. For all things are yours; Whether Paul, or Apollos, or Cephas, or the world, or life, or death, or things present, or things to come; all are yours; And ye are Christ's; and Christ is God's.

Ephesians 2:10: For we are his workmanship, created in Christ Jesus unto good works, which God hath before ordained that we should walk in them.

James 2:5: Hearken, my beloved brethren, hath not God chosen the poor of this world rich in faith, and heirs of the kingdom which he hath promised to them that love him?

We are His! We are His children. We are His heirs. We are His workmanship, being transformed and crafted, one thought at a time. We are who we think in our hearts to be. We are not beggars. We are not slaves. We have a position in the kingdom that gives us power and purpose. We have been chosen and have been given the opportunity to be heirs of *faith*, which opens the gates of the kingdom's riches, provision, and promises to us through the simplest action of seeking Him *first*, taking captive errant thoughts, and choosing to love the Lord and live each day according to His purpose. When we exchange our thoughts from the weak and beggarly to God's Word, we embrace and build a spiritual identity that far surpasses our limited human capacities and overcomes anything that would threaten to enslave us.

Seek first His kingdom, pursue His promises, and abide in His Word!

When we do:

- We will see ourselves as receivers and givers of the greatest gifts that can be given and received, because of the depth and width of our inheritance, held and distributed by our loving Father.
- We will see ourselves as masters of our own destiny, free of bondage and able to make a conscious choice of whom we serve and what we allow to influence our thoughts and actions.
- We will see ourselves as strong, courageous overcomers who confront and conquer obstacles that stand against the promises of our Father and the rule of His kingdom.

When we embrace our spiritual identity, we will see the kingdom of God, and the kingdom of God will be seen in us!

Reflection Questions

How has your understanding of your spiritual identity grown as you have read this book?

Have you identified any weak and beggarly thoughts or thoughts in your heart that don't belong that need to be rooted out and replaced so you can live in the inheritance God has given you? If so, what is your plan to quickly identify and reject those thoughts moving forward?

LEADER'S GUIDE

No More Beggars and Slaves

This book has been written to support both individual and group study. This section is designed to aid a group leader with additional questions and ideas to spark discussion and reflection.

General Tips

1. Read the chapter ahead of time and highlight key concepts. There are a lot of scriptures and content in each chapter, so focus on areas that you feel the most comfortable leading discussion on. You can also ask members to come with their favorite part or questions highlighted. If you'd like time to prepare, you may invite them to send questions in advance.

2. Answer the reflection questions for yourself. Some of the questions can be personal and challenging, and, as the group leader, you can help open dialogue by being willing to share your own insights.

3. Review the list of additional questions and choose one or two that might best fit the group's interests and facilitate discussion related to the theme that will have the most meaning for the group.

4. Each lesson includes some additional scriptures that are referenced in the chapter but aren't written out. As the leader, you can review these in advance and determine if it would be helpful to read one or more of the scriptures together. Members of the group can also be asked to review one of the scriptures in advance and to provide a summary to the group about how the scripture helped them further understand the theme of the chapter.

5. Songs often help convey concepts in scripture in a way that makes it easier to personalize and understand complex truths. As the group leader, you may want to find a song to play during the group session or invite others to speak about a song that they were reminded of as they read the chapter. A suggested song is listed for each chapter.

CHAPTER ONE

WHO I THINK I AM

Theme: Identity

Group Discussion Questions

1. An identity is the fact of being who or what a person or thing is. Our identity is framed by many things. Do you feel it is what has happened to you or what you think about the occurrence and how you react to it that has most influenced your view of yourself and the world?

2. How well do you feel you know yourself (what makes you tick and why you see yourself and the world the way you do)?

3. How well do you know God (His nature, desires, thoughts, and view of you and the world)?

4. Review the definitions of weak, beggarly, and bondage. Review the definition of elements (the beliefs that you build your identity upon). How can knowing these definitions help you evaluate your thoughts and how spiritually accurate they are?

5. Galatians 4:9 asks a very challenging question, "But now, after that ye have known God, or rather are known of God, how turn ye again to the weak and beggarly elements, whereunto ye desire again to be in bondage?" Have you ever felt yourself pulled back into old thoughts, mindsets, or habits that are inconsistent with the new identity you have in Christ? Is it easy to recognize weak and beggarly elements in your life so you can overcome them?

6. What do you already know about what scripture says about your identity in Christ? Do you ever have trouble convincing yourself

that what scriptures in the Bible say are *true about you* because of conflicting thoughts you hold about yourself?

Go-Deeper Scriptures

- Romans 12:1–2
- Isaiah 55:8–9
- Ephesians 2:2–3

Group Review of the Reflection Questions

Where has your concept of self come from?

How much have you invested in developing your knowledge of your spiritual identity in Christ?

How is your spiritual identity reflected

- in your life every day?
- in times of trouble?
- in your use of time?
- in your self-talk?
- in your interactions with others?

Possible song to share or meditate on: "Who You Say I Am," words and music by Ben Fielding and Reuben Morgan.

CHAPTER TWO

I AM ROYALTY

Theme: Inheritance

Group Discussion Questions

1. We often hear about the concept of being part of the family of God, but has that ever led you to fully envision yourself, not only as a child but also as an heir responsible for protecting and advancing the kingdom as well as receiving its inheritance? Do you see the difference between being a child and being an heir?

2. Compare and contrast the roles, responsibilities, rights, and privileges of your earthly (born or adopted into) family and being reborn into the family of God and heir to His kingdom. What roles, responsibilities, rights, and privileges do you have in God's kingdom, and how is that similar or different from your earthly family?

3. Within the text, it asks, "Are you ready to move from being a child to an heir who understands the rights, responsibilities, and benefits of the position given to you upon coming into the family of God?" What do you think it would take to make that change?

4. How can you "affirm your spiritual identity" more consistently, reflecting the DNA of God the Father and reflecting the values and promises of the kingdom of God?

5. How does it feel to know you are a joint heir with Christ? Does it shift the way you view yourself? Does it inspire you to learn more about His position and power and to build a stronger relationship with Him?

6. Based on Galatians 3:28–29, what does it mean to "be an heir according to a promise"? Are you ready to live out the promises of the inheritance?

Go-Deeper Scriptures

- 2 Corinthians 5:17
- Philippians 2:1–8
- Ephesians 2:1–10
- Matthew 25

Group Review of the Reflection Questions

Did you learn anything new about being a child of God from this chapter? How can you deepen the parent-child relationship with Him?

What aspects of your spiritual inheritance did you already know about?

What parts of your inheritance do you want to learn more about?

What can you do with this information to build a stronger spiritual identity as one who does everything "with" and "in" Christ who is sharing his position with you as joint heir?

Possible song to share or meditate on: "Inheritance" by Dameon Aranda, JT Murrell, Matt Maher and Mia Fieldes.

CHAPTER THREE

No Beggin', Just Believin'

Theme: Self-Actualization

Group Discussion Questions

1. The first pages of this chapter describe the beggarly mindset. Can you think of other examples or other results of entertaining beggarly thoughts?
2. There are several promises and blessings listed in scripture. Have you ever considered these as benefits listed in God's will that are reserved for His heirs? If it is a new concept, how might it change the way you read scripture?
3. Within the text, it asks, "Have you embraced the gift of being you?" You were uniquely given talents, gifts, and abilities to get what you need for yourself and for your family and to serve God. Are you embracing your design as one way for Him to supply all of your needs?
4. Salvation is to be made whole, complete in our design and enabling us to find what we need in Him. The next time you experience an area of lack, how might you proceed, knowing that He has made you to benefit from the work of your hands and to partner with Him for an expectation of success from both spiritual and physical resources?
5. What is the difference between begging and making a personal, selective, and expectant request of God?

Go-Deeper Scriptures

- Hebrews 11:1–3
- 2 Peter 1:8–10
- Hebrews 13:20–21

Group Review of the Reflection Questions

Do you tend to focus more on lack, gaps, and needs in your life than on your spiritual position and privileges available as a joint heir with Christ?

How can knowing more about your spiritual identity lead you to being stronger and bolder, even in times of need?

When you go to Christ with a request, is it

- personal (reflective of your relationship with Him)?
- selective (because you know He is the only one who can)?
- expectant (with a clear outcome based on scripture in mind)?

Possible song to share or meditate on: "Believe for It" by CeCe Winans.

CHAPTER FOUR

WHY ARE YOU ASKIN' AGAIN?

Theme: Trust + Knowledge = Confidence

Group Discussion Questions

1. Within the text, it states, "A promise is an announcement and pledge providing divine assurance of good." Promises are pledges of God's will made available to all heirs. Can you think of three to four of your favorite scriptures and recognize the promise within them?

2. Once you know God's will, you can shift from a yes/no question of Him into a declaration of faith based on what *you* know about the Word of God, what *your part* is in receiving the promise, and what *you have the faith to believe and act upon.* How might this change the way you approach prayer?

3. Have you ever considered the conditions (our part, the "if" of scriptures) that are part of receiving the promises in the will of God? Review your favorite scriptures to find *your* part and the work of faith you will need to do to become heir to the promise.

4. What does "faith without works is dead" mean to you, and how have you applied it to your Christian walk and prayer life? How do you "keep faith alive" while you are waiting for what is currently hoped for and unseen to become seen?

Go-Deeper Scriptures

- Isaiah 40:28–31
- 1 Peter 2:9–12
- Psalm 27:7–14
- Mark 8:34–35

Group Review of the Reflection Questions

What should you do to learn what God's will is before you ask Him for something?

Did you know that most promises of God included things for *you* to do to receive? Have you ever seen and focused on the conditions of the promises before?

How might you increase demonstration of your faith through works that prove your confidence in God's promises?

Possible song to share or meditate on: "Yes and Amen" by Tony Brown, Chris McClamey, Nate Moore; lyrics © Bethel Music Publishing.

CHAPTER FIVE

YOU'VE GOT PLENTY TO SHARE

Theme: Generosity

Group Discussion Questions

1. Have you ever experienced how opening your hands to give has better positioned you to receive, or have you acted on the encouragement to "give out of need"? What was the result?

2. Since God is a giver and we are part of His family and share His values, what can we do to bring more of His nature into us and more of His kingdom into the world?

3. Tithing is an act of trust and a command given to build the nature of giving within us. If you have built the act of tithing into your lifestyle, what have the benefits been? If you have struggled with establishing the practice, what can you do to make it a consistent part of your lifestyle?

4. Matthew 10:9 says, "Freely you have been given, freely you must give." What does this mean to you, and how would someone looking at your life "from the outside in" see the value reflected?

5. The text says, "Your design will be revealed in you the more you give yourself to the life God has called you to live." How do you give yourself to God so you can learn more about your calling and what you have to give to the kingdom and this world?

Go-Deeper Scriptures

- Luke 6:37–3
- Psalm 37:21–24
- Luke 10:38–42

Group Review of the Reflection Questions

Have you ever felt fearful to give because you thought you didn't have enough for your own needs? If so, how did you overcome that? If that is a current concern, how can you address the fear of lack and become a giver of 10 percent?

What opportunities did God give you to share your time, talents, or treasure generously in the last year? How did you respond?

Possible song to share or meditate on: "Give to the Lord," words and music by Ron Kenoly.

CHAPTER SIX

MY WILL, MY LIFE

Theme: Self-Determination

Group Discussion Questions

1. Christ calls us brethren. Are there choices you are making about your finances, church life, fellowship, habits, service, study, prayer, and personal growth that are intentionally meant to align your will with Christ and the values of the family of God?

2. There are several people we may choose to be subject to. Children yield to parents. Workers yield to a supervisor's direction. God calls us to respect all leaders and roles of authority. In fact, Christ willingly submitted to the Father. Whom do you yield to, and why have you *chosen* to yield? Whom do you refuse to yield to, and why?

3. We can live life reactively or intentionally. It takes an intentional focus to think and act in accordance with our spiritual identity and to do things differently from what might come naturally based on old patterns or worldly expectations. How have you chosen to be different from what you otherwise would be as your understanding and relationship with God has grown?

4. The text says that "we must use our will to choose each day what we will allow ourselves to be subject to and what and whom we will submit to." Have you underestimated how much control you have over your thoughts, choices, and life? Do you want to use your powerful will to take control over old thoughts and habits and be more spiritually focused?

Go-Deeper Scriptures

- Genesis 1:26–28
- 2 Timothy 2:20–26
- Joshua 24:11–28
- James 4:1–10

Group Review of the Reflection Questions

Do you ever feel like life is "out of control"? How do you respond in those moments to regain a sense of God-given power and control?

How do you or can you use your will to be more intentional about how you live your life and whom you serve with it?

Possible song to share or meditate on: "I Choose Joy," music and lyrics by Larnelle Harris.

CHAPTER SEVEN

CHOOSING MY MASTER

Theme: Service

Group Discussion Questions

1. Within the text, it states, "Choosing a Lord and Master is a crucial element of our spiritual identity because it pulls us beyond the boundaries of self and gives us a place in a kingdom that has deep meaning and eternal reward." Have you been experiencing this sense of service and connection to something larger than yourself? Are you looking for more of it?

2. When we begin to see Christ as Lord, we begin to seek to do His will and serve the Father by caring for one another and looking for ways to bring His love and provision to others. Has your desire to serve grown or changed over time?

3. We receive rewards and benefits from many things. Minimally, an occupation provides income, if not purpose and camaraderie. Philanthropy provides us with a way to support people and causes that matter. Are there opportunities God has introduced into your life that you haven't yet taken advantage of that could be key to receiving the full inheritance He has for you?

4. Romans 1:25 shares that we can risk worshiping or serving something God created instead of the Creator. Many people who do not recognize God may still do good acts of service or take extra care to protect the earth. How do you keep your service to the Master focused on the will of God and the good work He has made you to do?

Go-Deeper Scriptures

- Luke 15:11–32
- Matthew 4:1–11

Group Review of the Reflection Questions

As you look back over the last year, has your life been a clear reflection of the Master you serve?

Have you considered yourself a disciple or follower of Christ as your Master? If so, how has your relationship with your Master been developed? How is He kept in the position of Lord over your life?

How can you be more intentional about using your time, talents, and treasure to honor the one who purchased you and redeemed you from a life of bondage to self and sin?

Possible song to share or meditate on: "Make Room," written by Joshua Neil Farro, Evelyn Braun Heideriqui, Rebekah Erin White, Lucas Salles Cortazio; featuring Elyssa Smith and Community Music.

CHAPTER EIGHT

NO MORE STRONGHOLDS!

Theme: Overcoming

Group Discussion Questions

1. There are several tools and techniques in scripture that teach us how to defeat thoughts that weaken us. How can you effectively fight the good fight of faith described in 1 Timothy 6:12?

2. The text says, "We are equipped to set our beliefs on our ability to prevail and then act quickly in alignment with that belief." If you had an expectation to win every time you fought, how would that change your perspective? Do you see every faith fight as an opportunity to taste victory?

3. What is your experience "putting on the armor of God" as described in Ephesians 6:10–18? This scripture helps us set our heart and mind to be strong, protected, and confident no matter what "fiery dart" is launched. What does it take for you to get your thoughts to align with God's Word so you can stand strong against anything that comes your way? How might you use this practice in the future?

4. While we have been made new through Christ, we continue to have a natural/carnal nature. What can you do to handle this old nature better and learn to be more spiritually aware, building up your spiritual nature to lead and manage the old? How might you "take revenge" on any stronghold that has effectively held you back in the past?

Go-Deeper Scriptures

- Galatians 2:20–21
- Revelation 12:7–12
- James 2:14–26
- Philippians 4:1–19

Group Review of the Reflection Questions

Are there certain negative thoughts about yourself that keep rising up, taking a higher position of influence in your mind than they should?

How do you identify them?

How do you take them captive, cast them down, and replace them with spiritual truth?

What areas do you feel like you are an overcomer, and in what areas do you feel like you need to build your faith to experience confidence and assurance that you can and will prevail?

What action will you take to build your faith in those areas?

Possible song to share or meditate on: "No Longer Slaves," words and music by Johnathan David and Melissa Helser; © Bethel Music.

CHAPTER NINE

GREAT IN GOD

Theme: Mind Management

Group Discussion Questions

1. It is a bold challenge to "seek ye first the kingdom of God" knowing that making something first includes giving it the highest ranking in time, order, placement, and importance. What are very practical steps for reordering the position of a spiritual focus in your life?

2. Our will and our thoughts are powerful. We have the responsibility and ability to think more soberly (moderately take in information so we can assess it) and to be intentional in the actions that follow. This is especially important when we are under stress. Think of the last time you didn't manage your thoughts soberly or act intentionally. What was the outcome? If you could redo the situation, how might you manage your mind for a better outcome?

3. How can our mind management and living out of our position of strength and confidence become a good witness to others who want to understand the benefits of being a child of God? How can embracing our spiritual identity and all the love, power, and provision God has for us be something that draws others into understanding the inheritance of God better?

4. 1 Corinthians 3 outlines many of the elements discussed in this book, highlighting the rewards God has as part of the inheritance promised to His heirs. After reading the chapter, what part did you find particularly inspirational? Particularly challenging?

Go-Deeper Scriptures

- 1 Timothy 4:8–16
- Joshua 1:6–9
- Hebrews 2
- Philippians 2

Group Review of the Reflection Questions

How has your understanding of your spiritual identity grown as you have read this book?

Have you identified any weak and beggarly thoughts or thoughts in your heart that don't belong that need to be rooted out and replaced so you can live in the inheritance God has given you? If so, what is your plan to quickly identify and reject those thoughts moving forward?

Possible song to share or meditate on: "First Things First," words and music by Consumed by Fire.

Printed in the United States
by Baker & Taylor Publisher Services